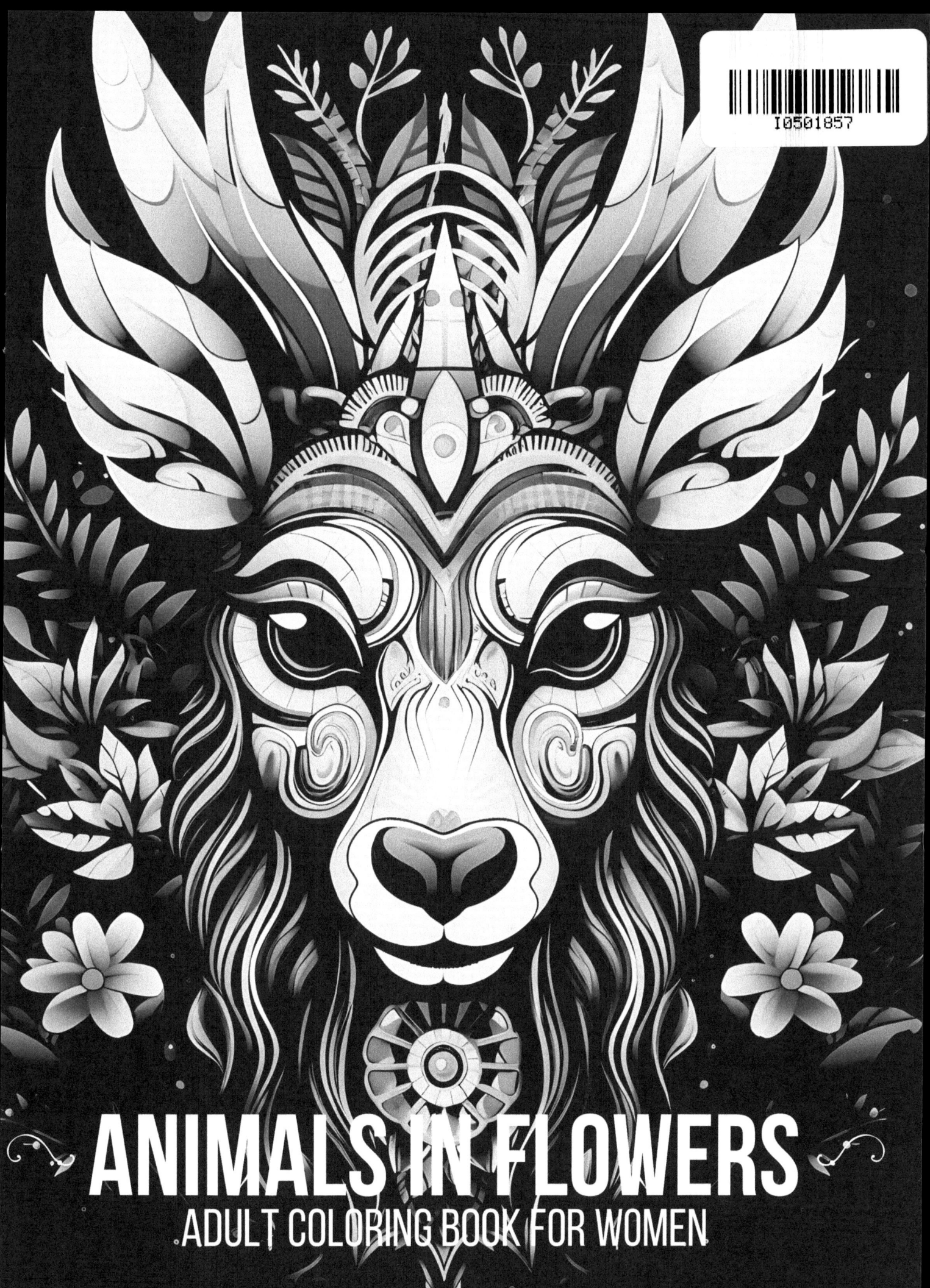

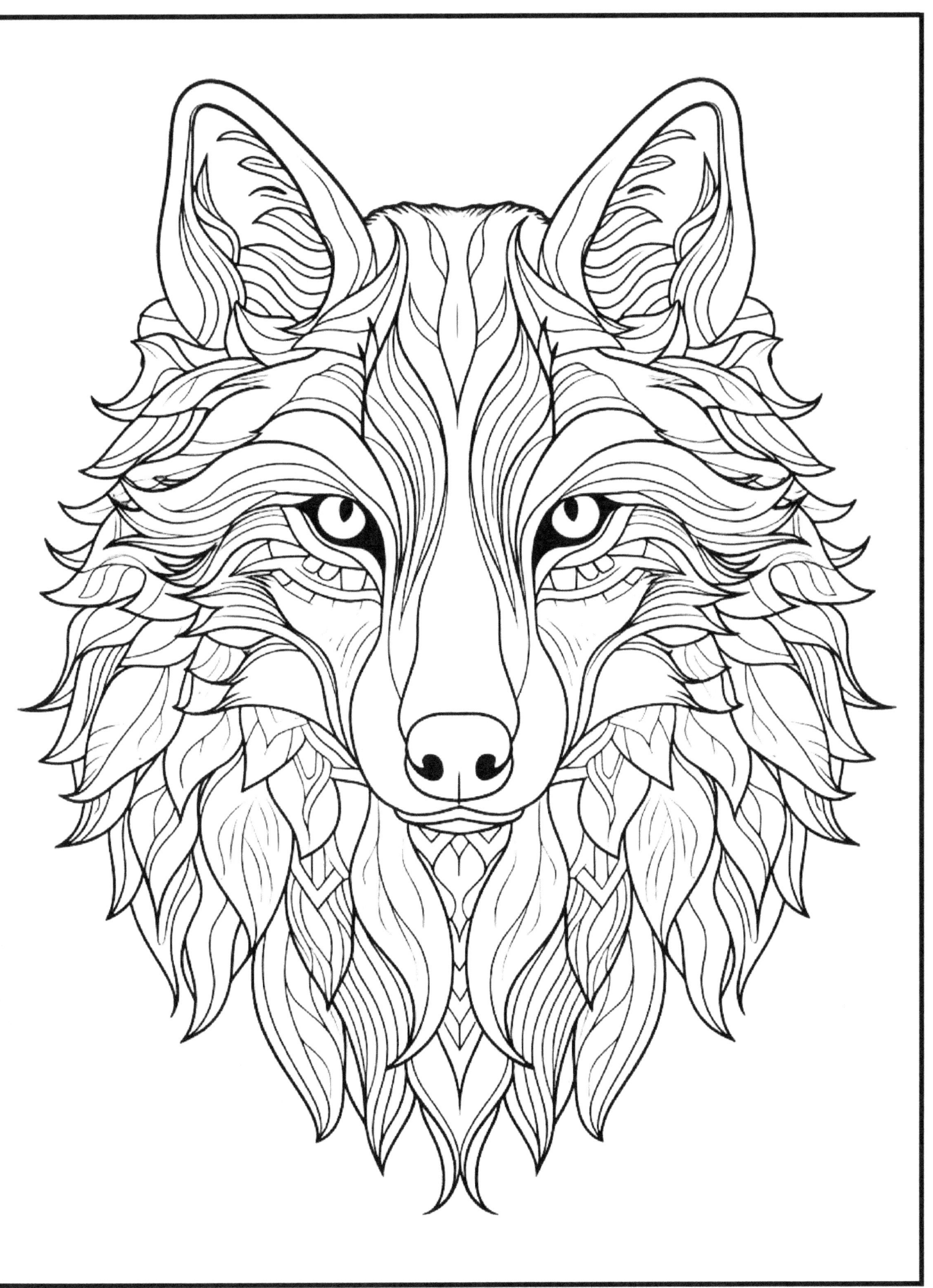

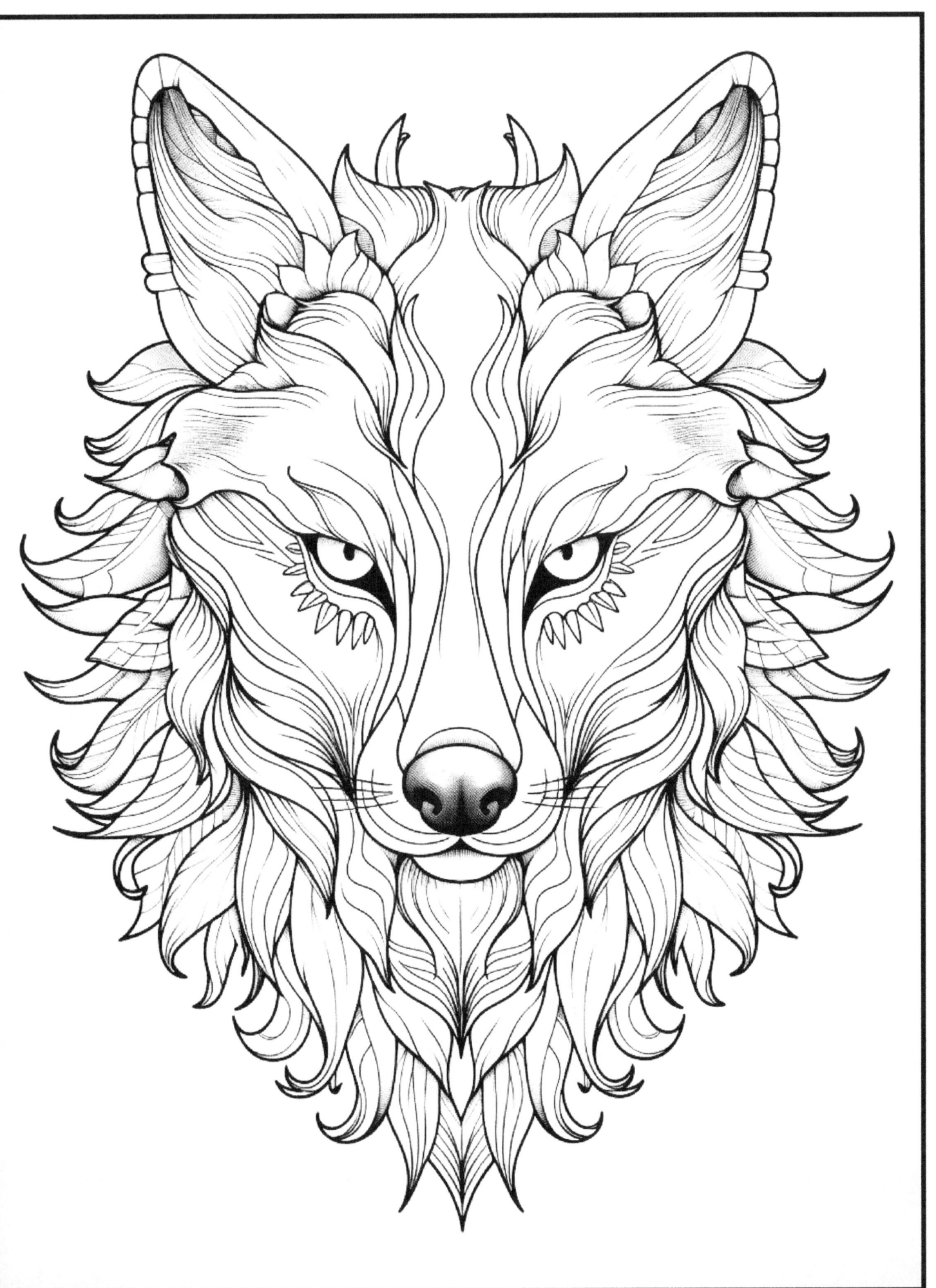

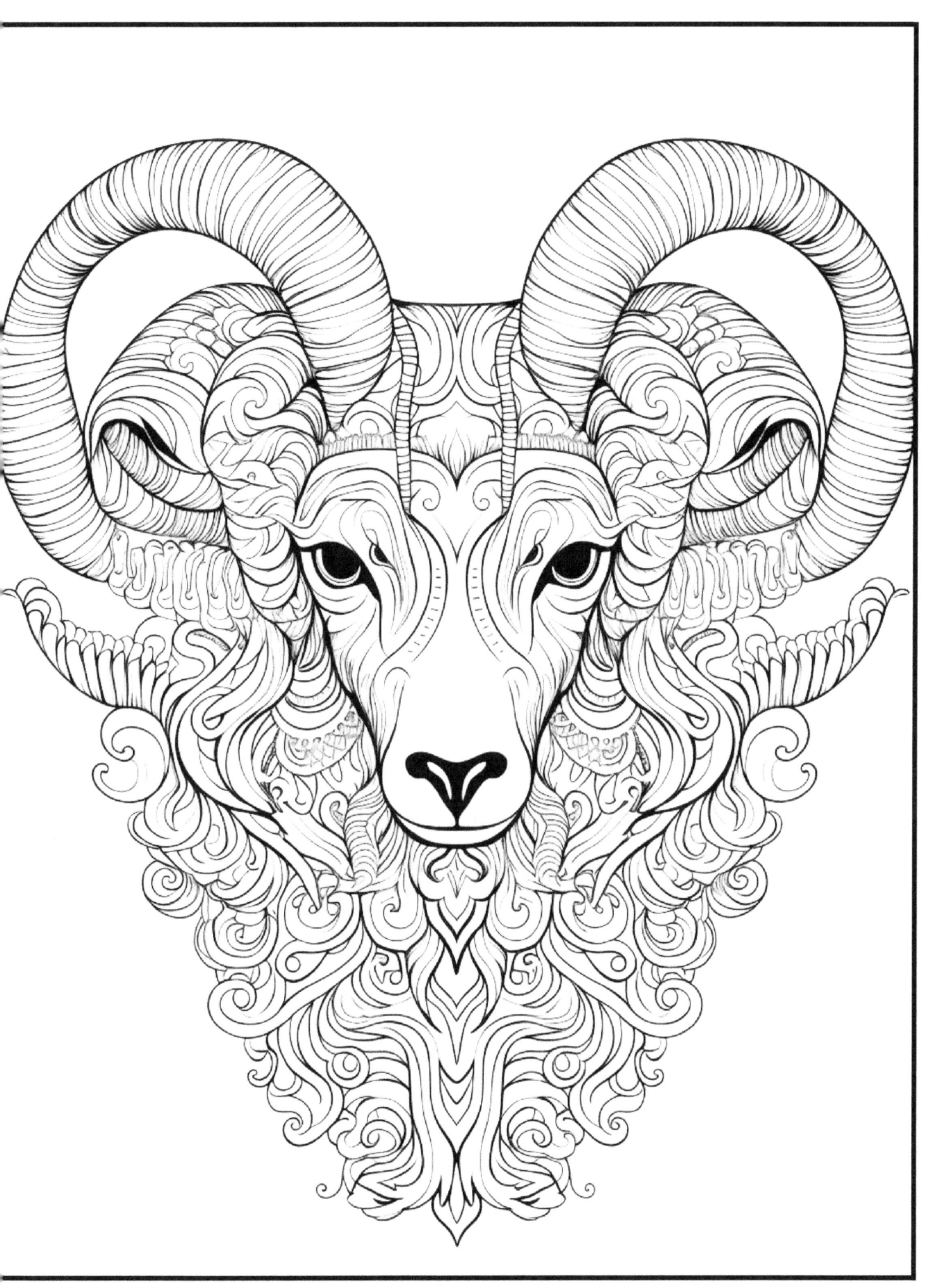

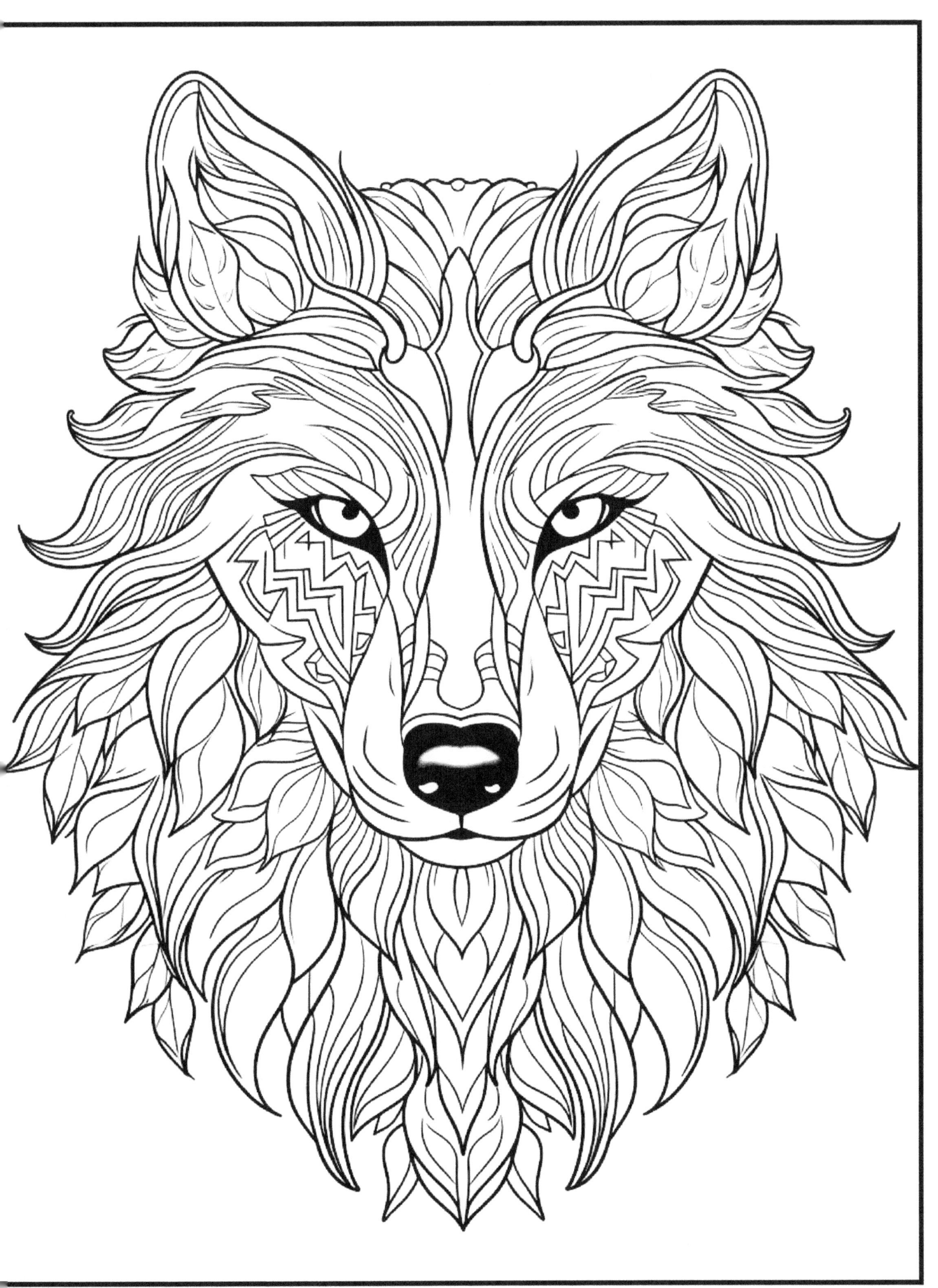

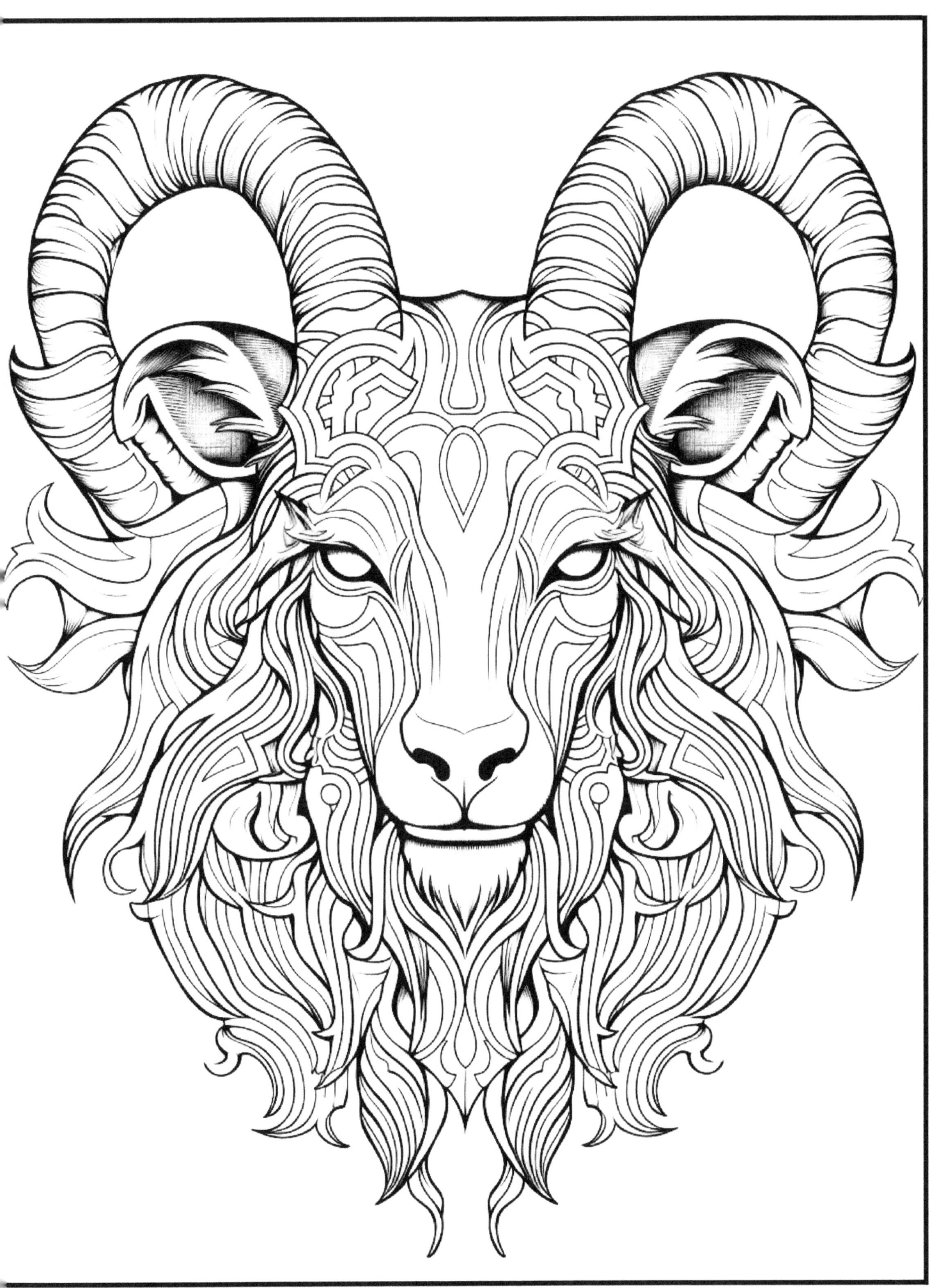

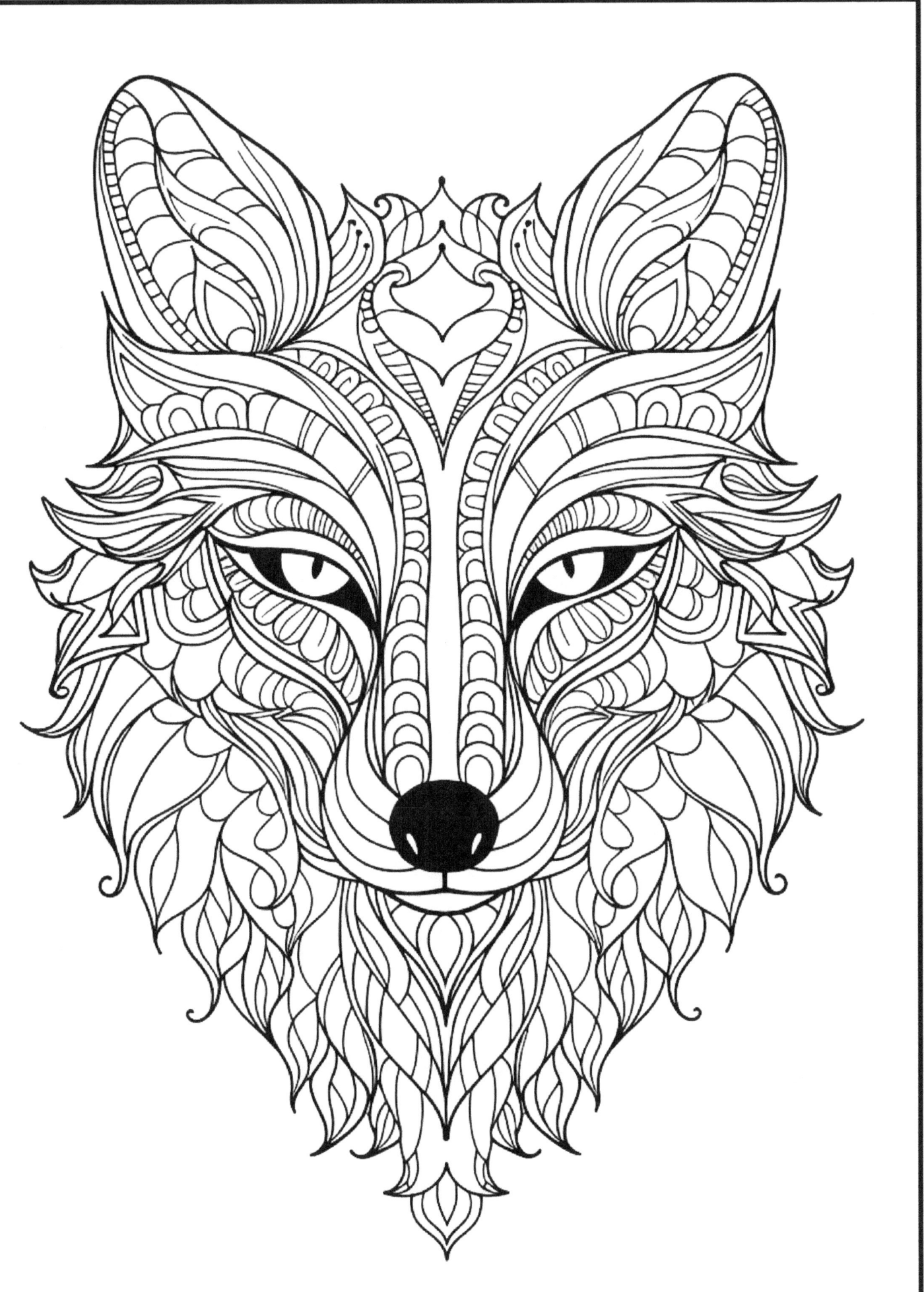

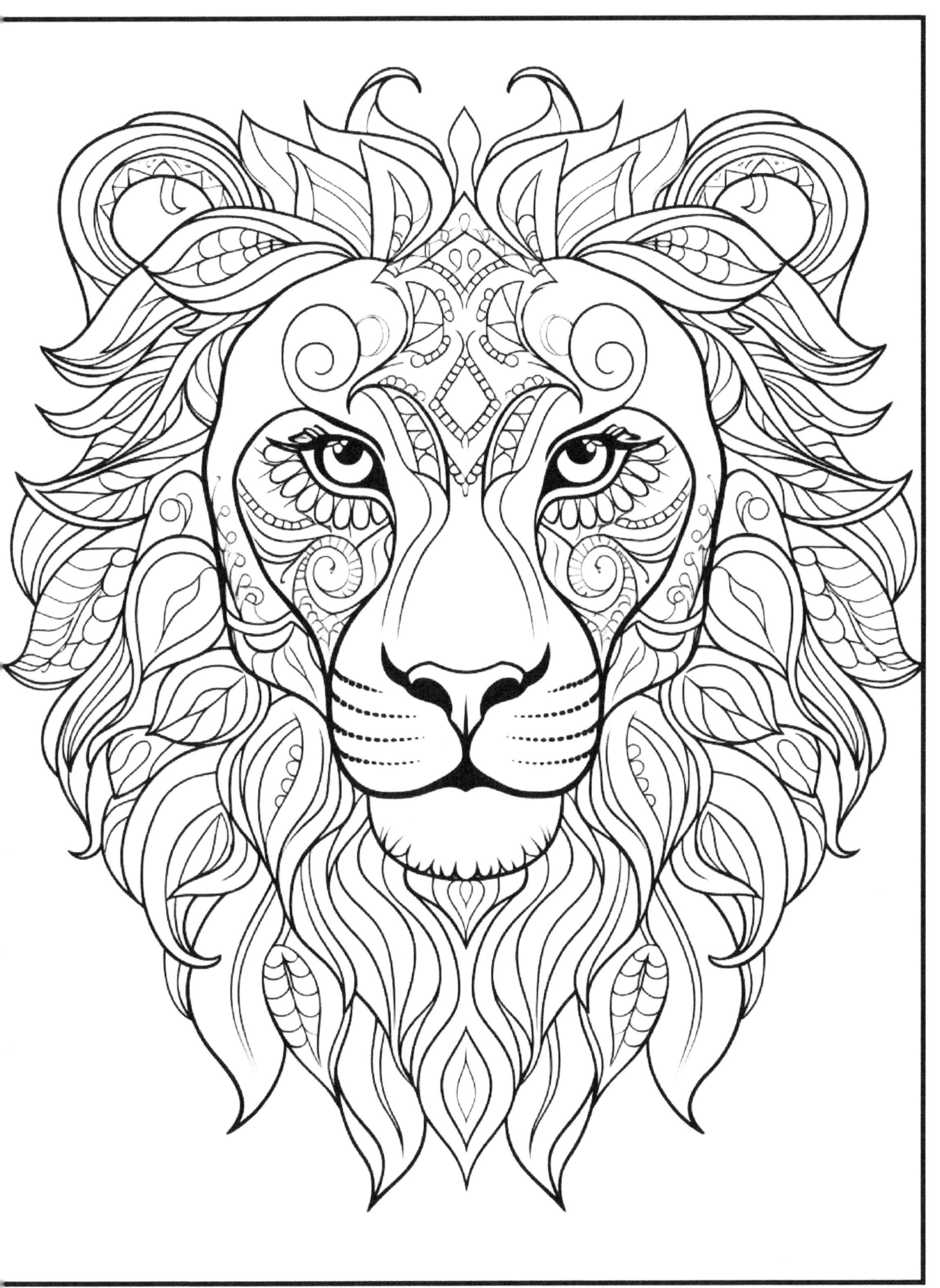

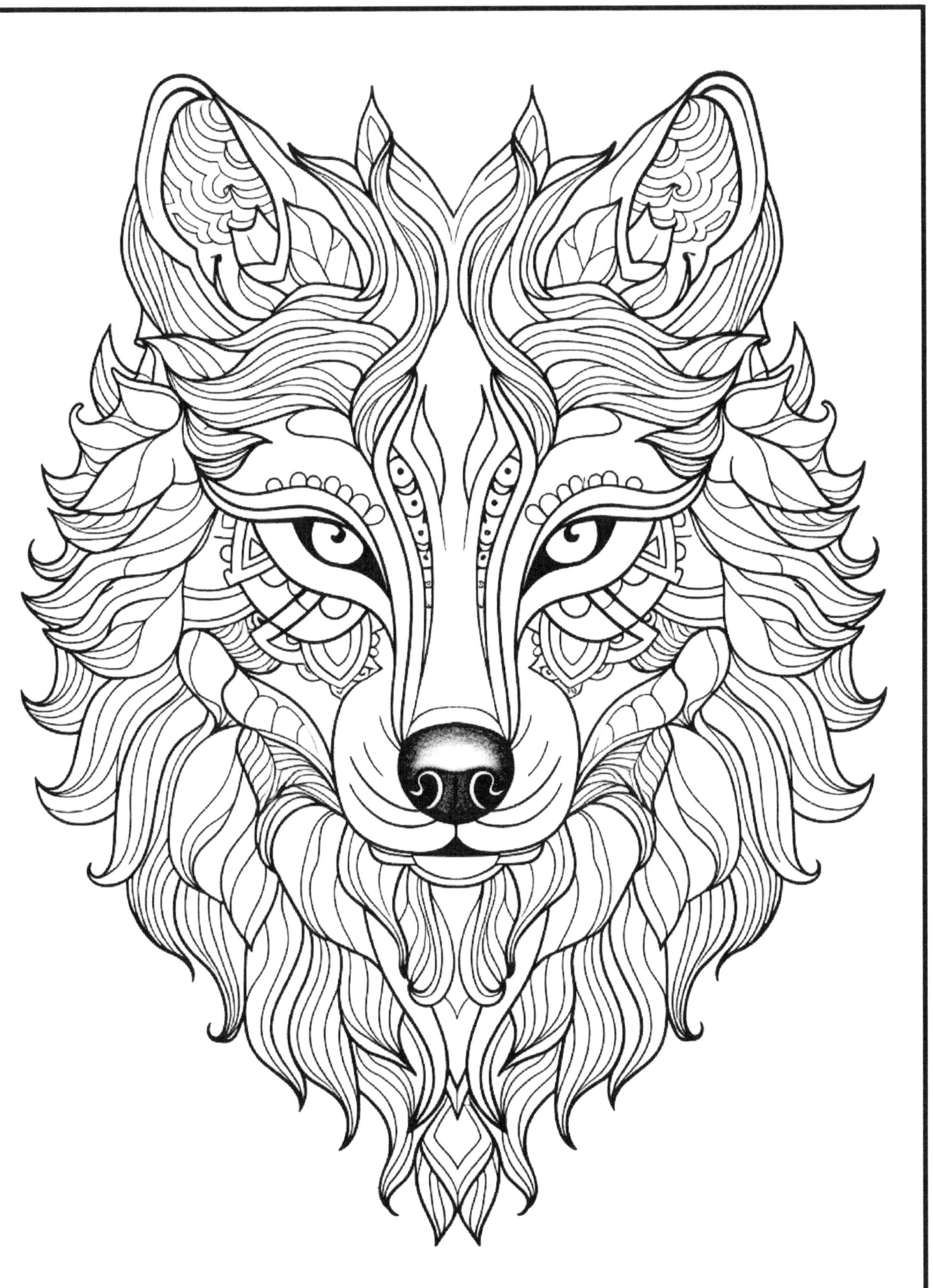

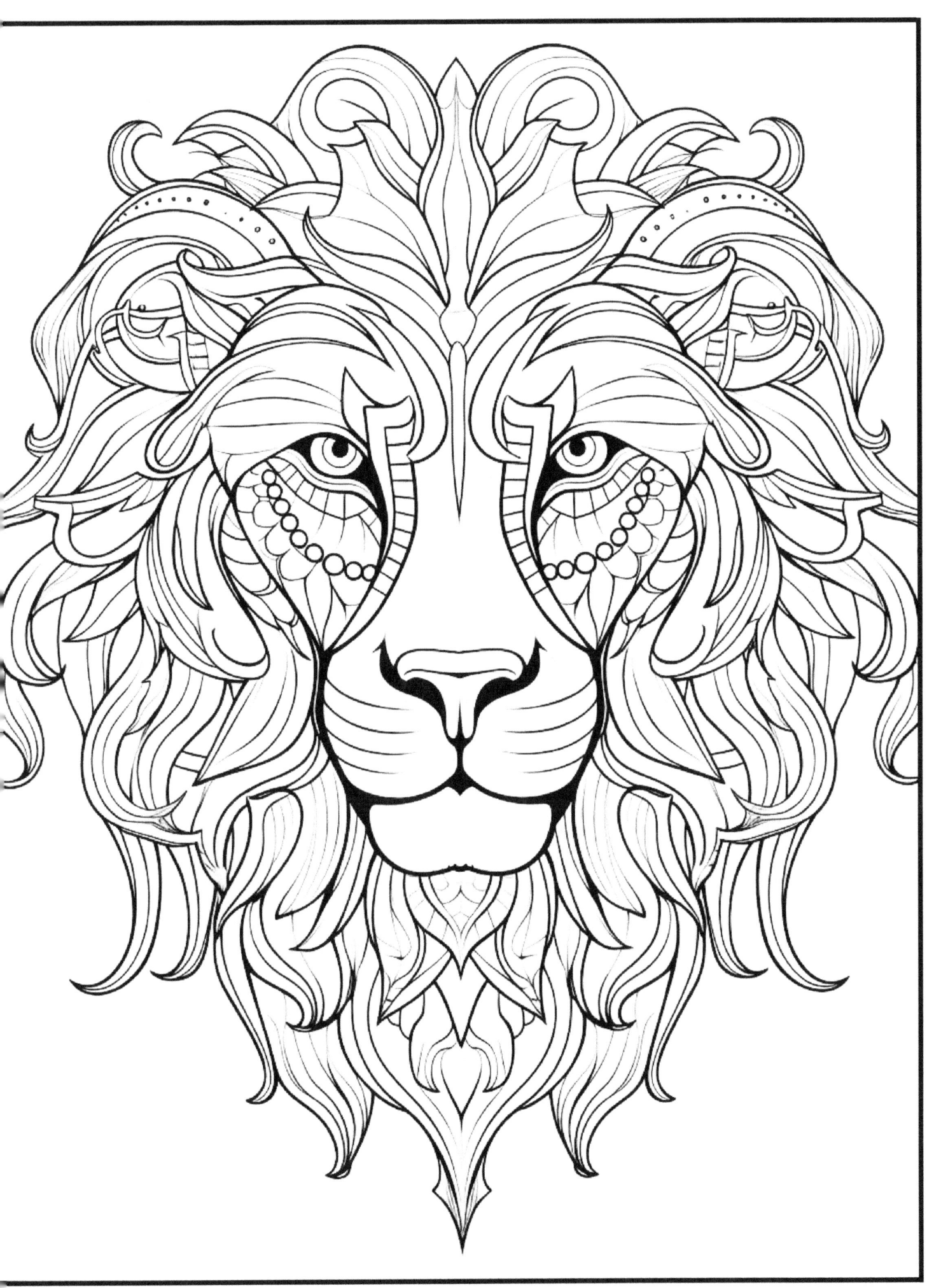

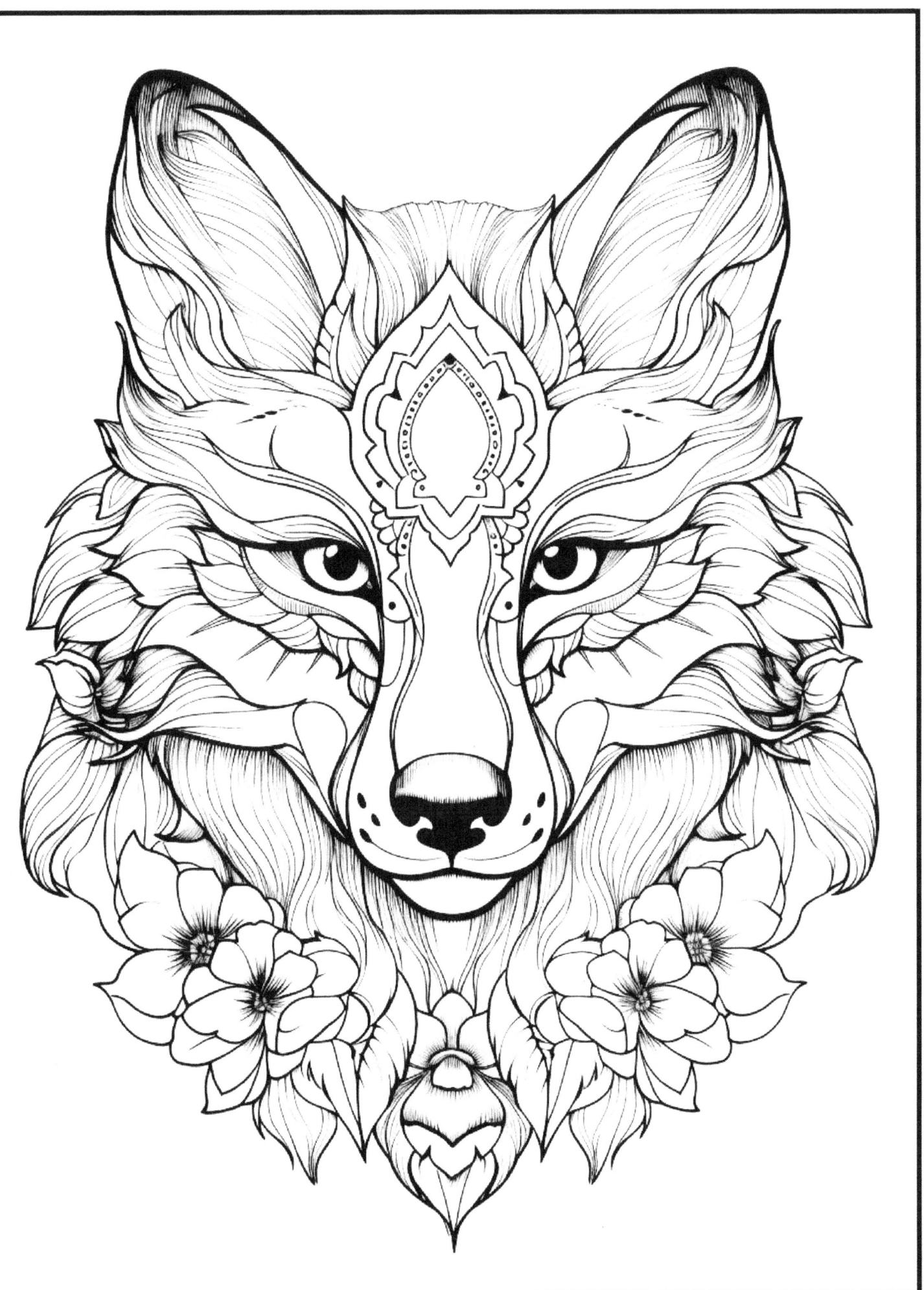

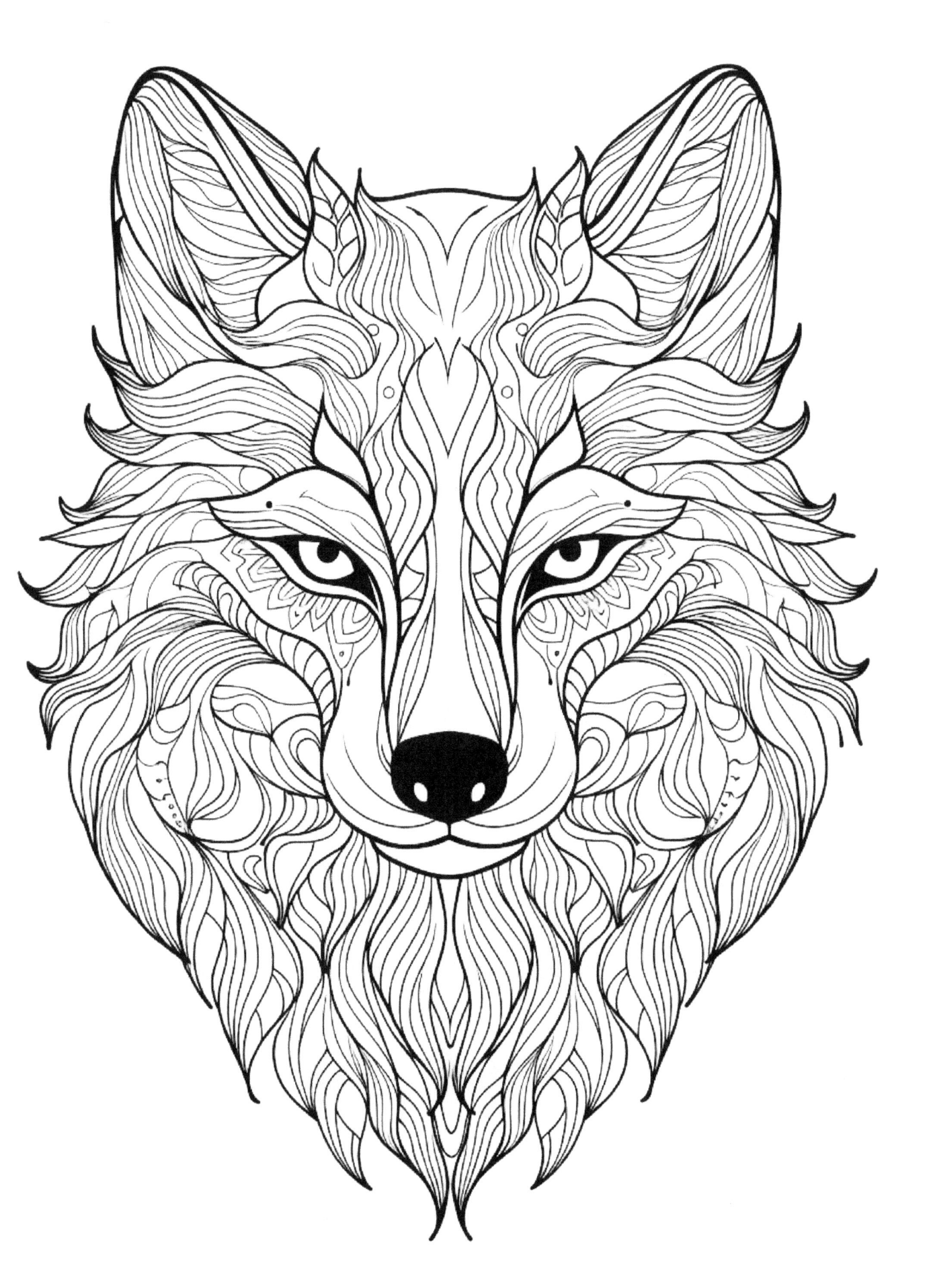

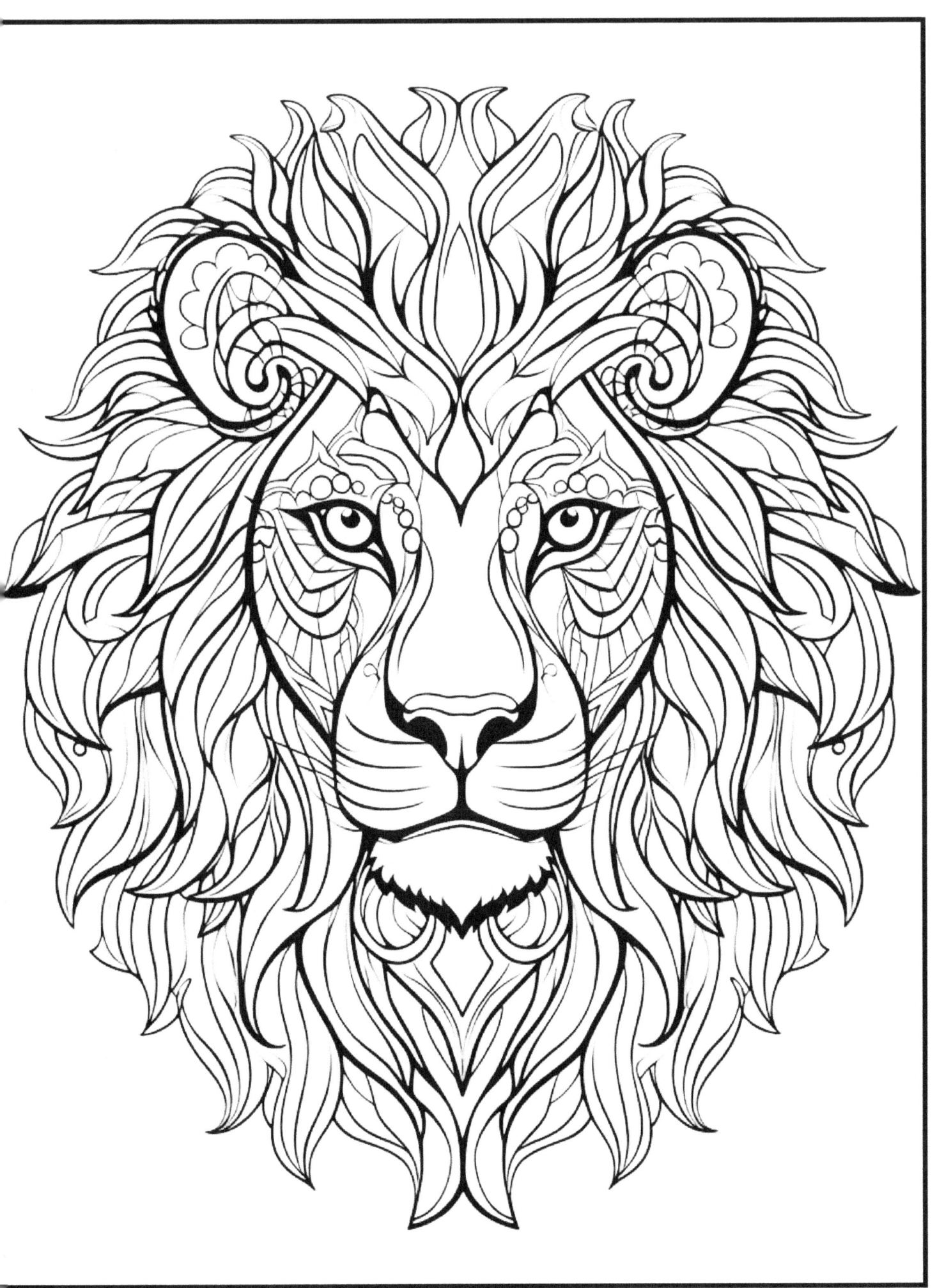

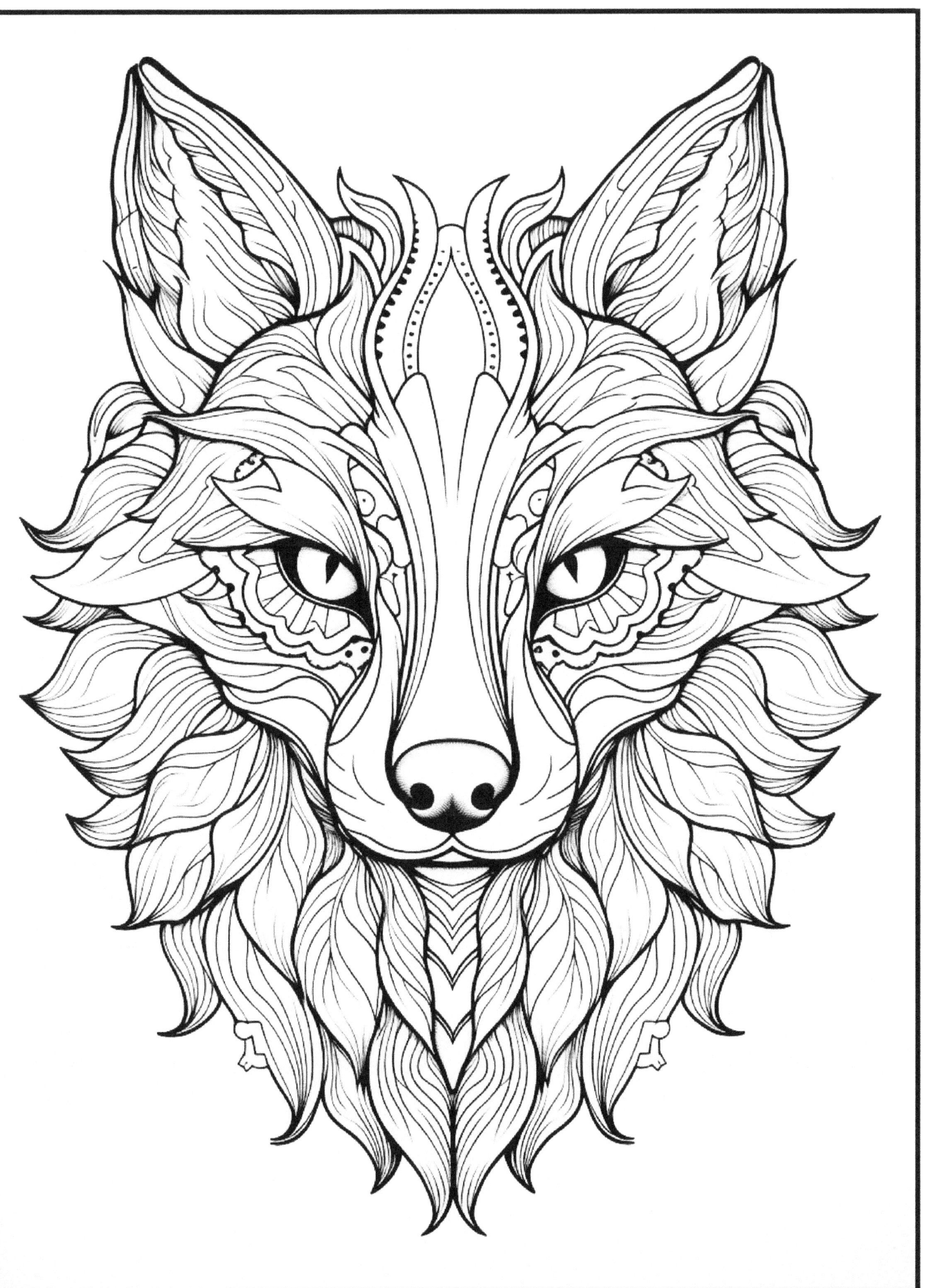

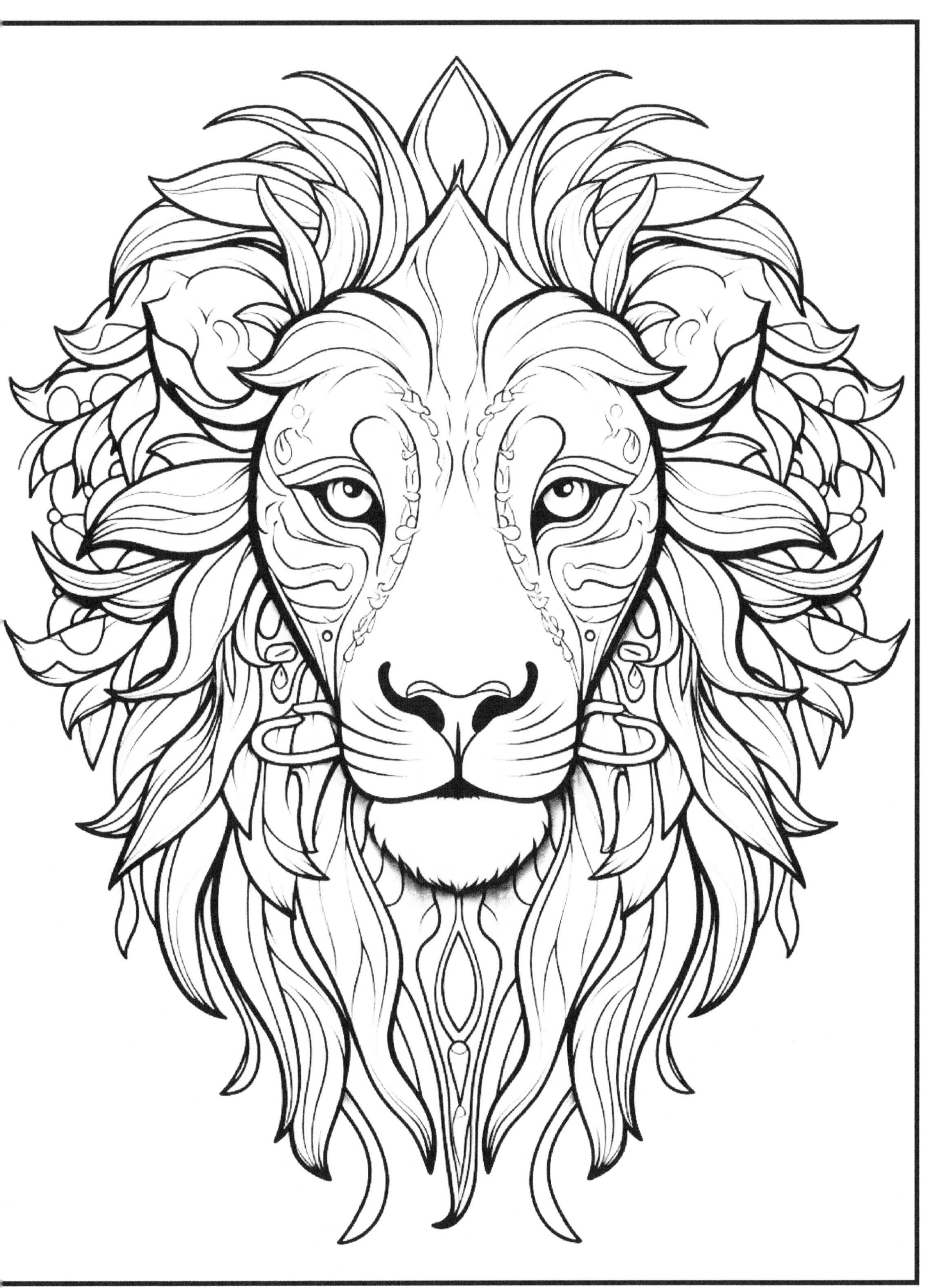

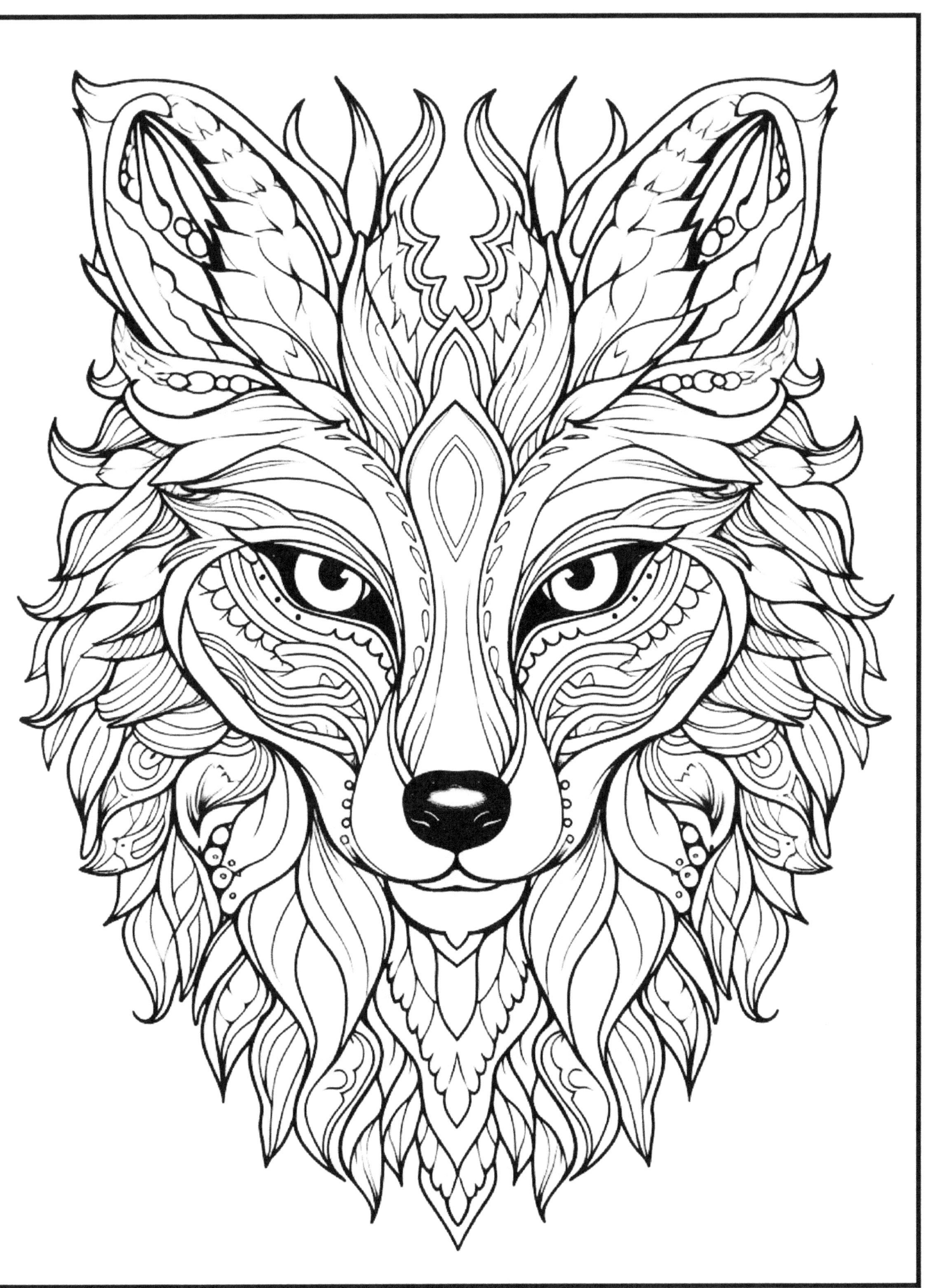

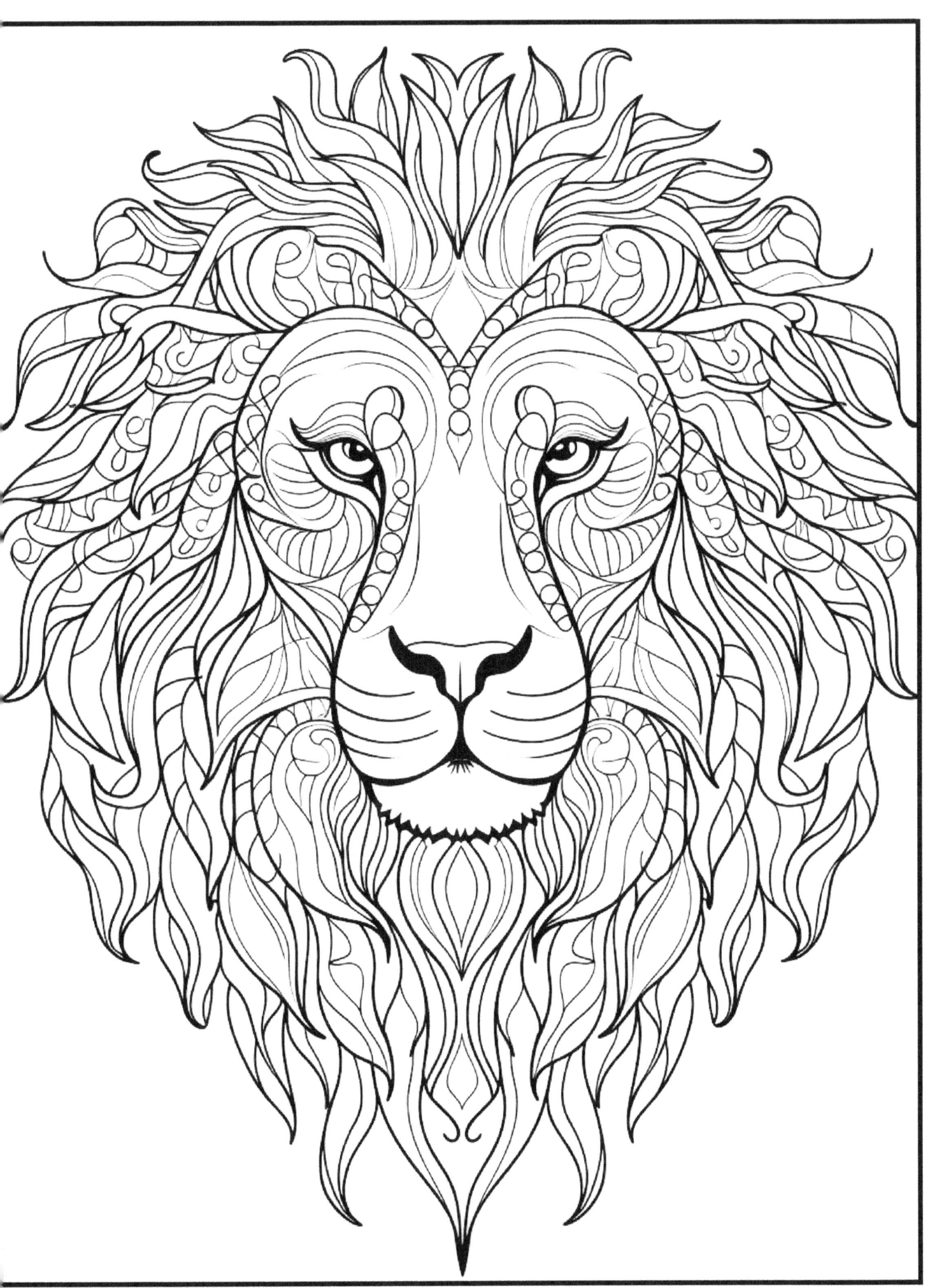

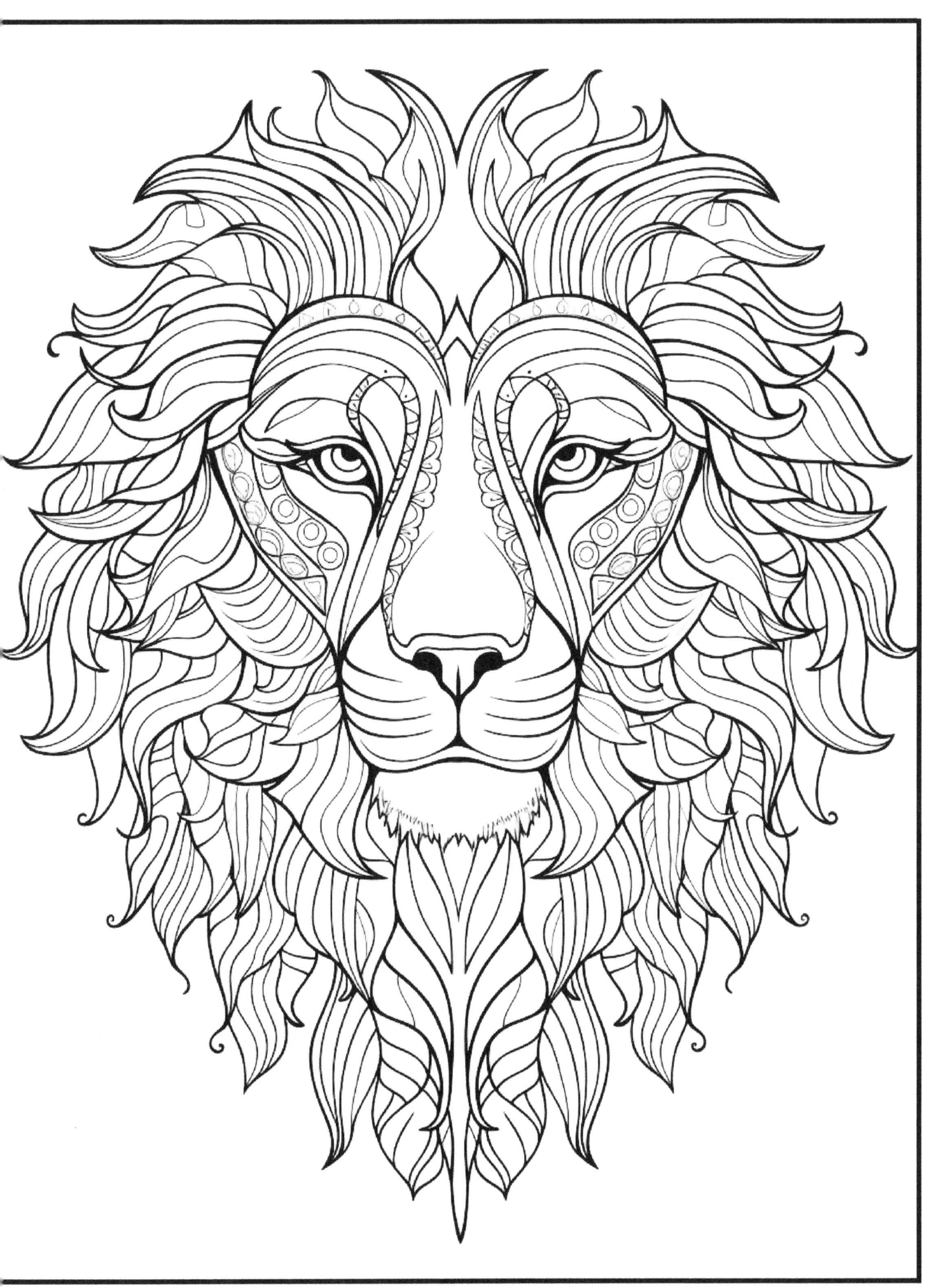

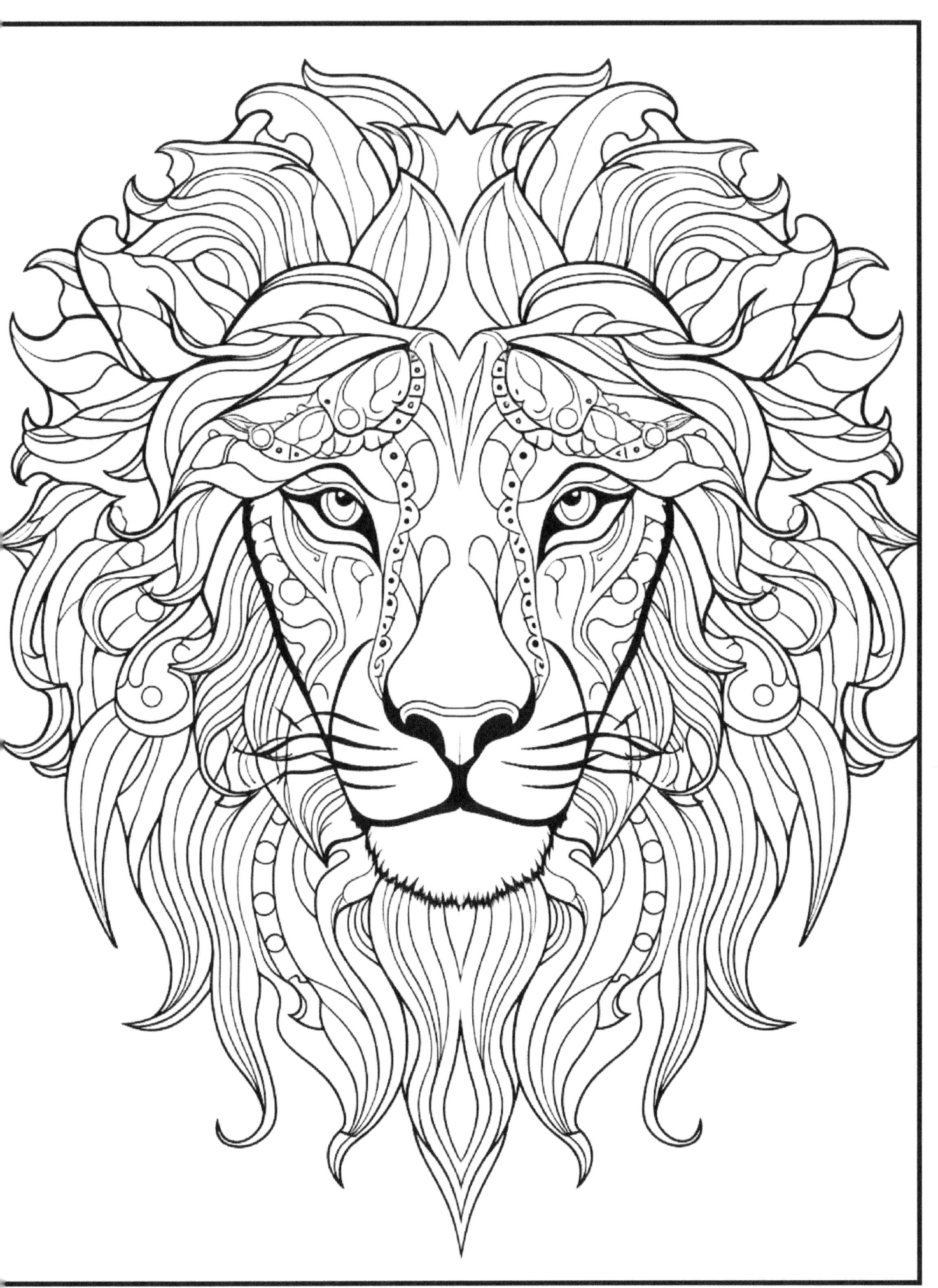

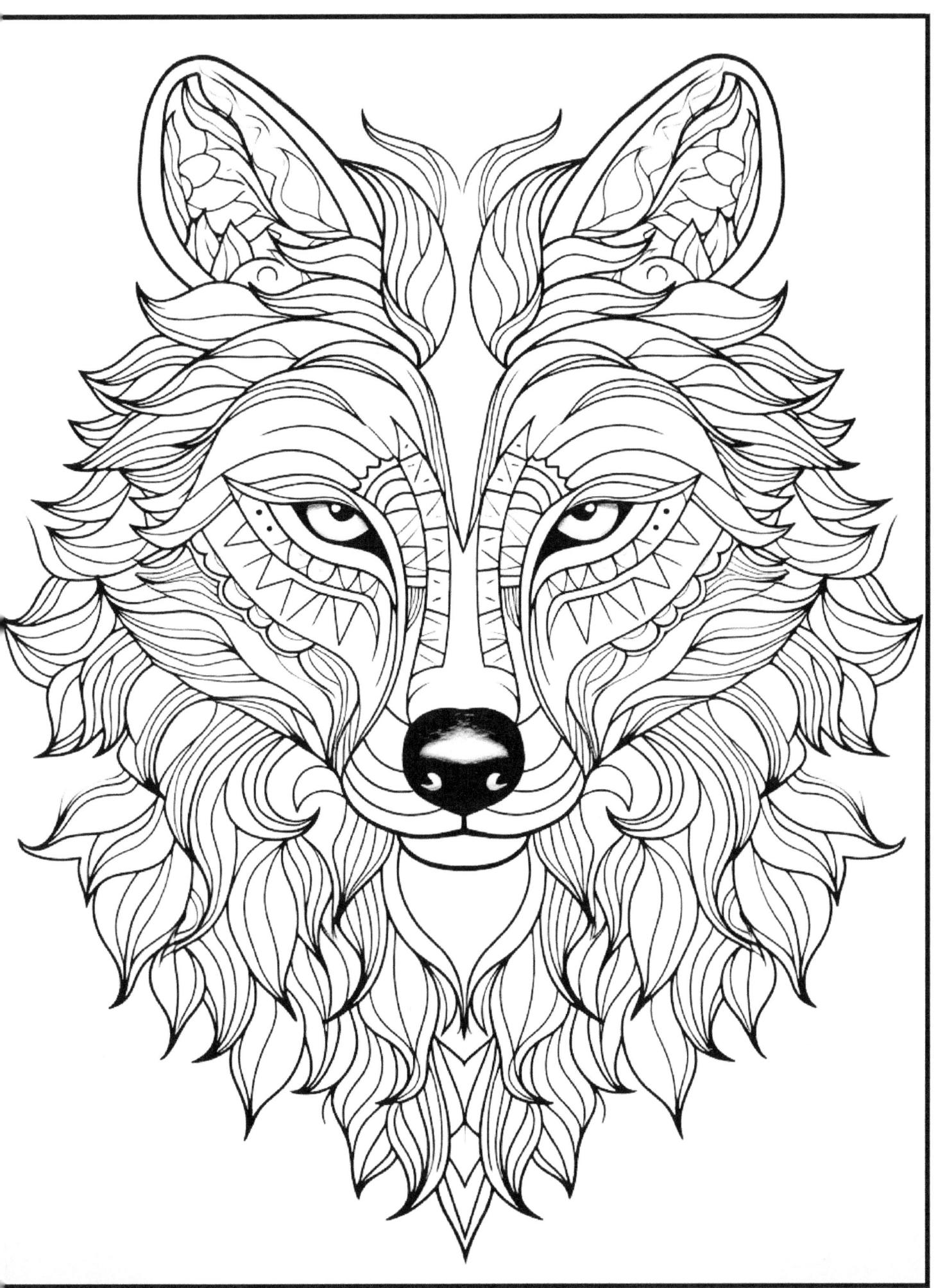

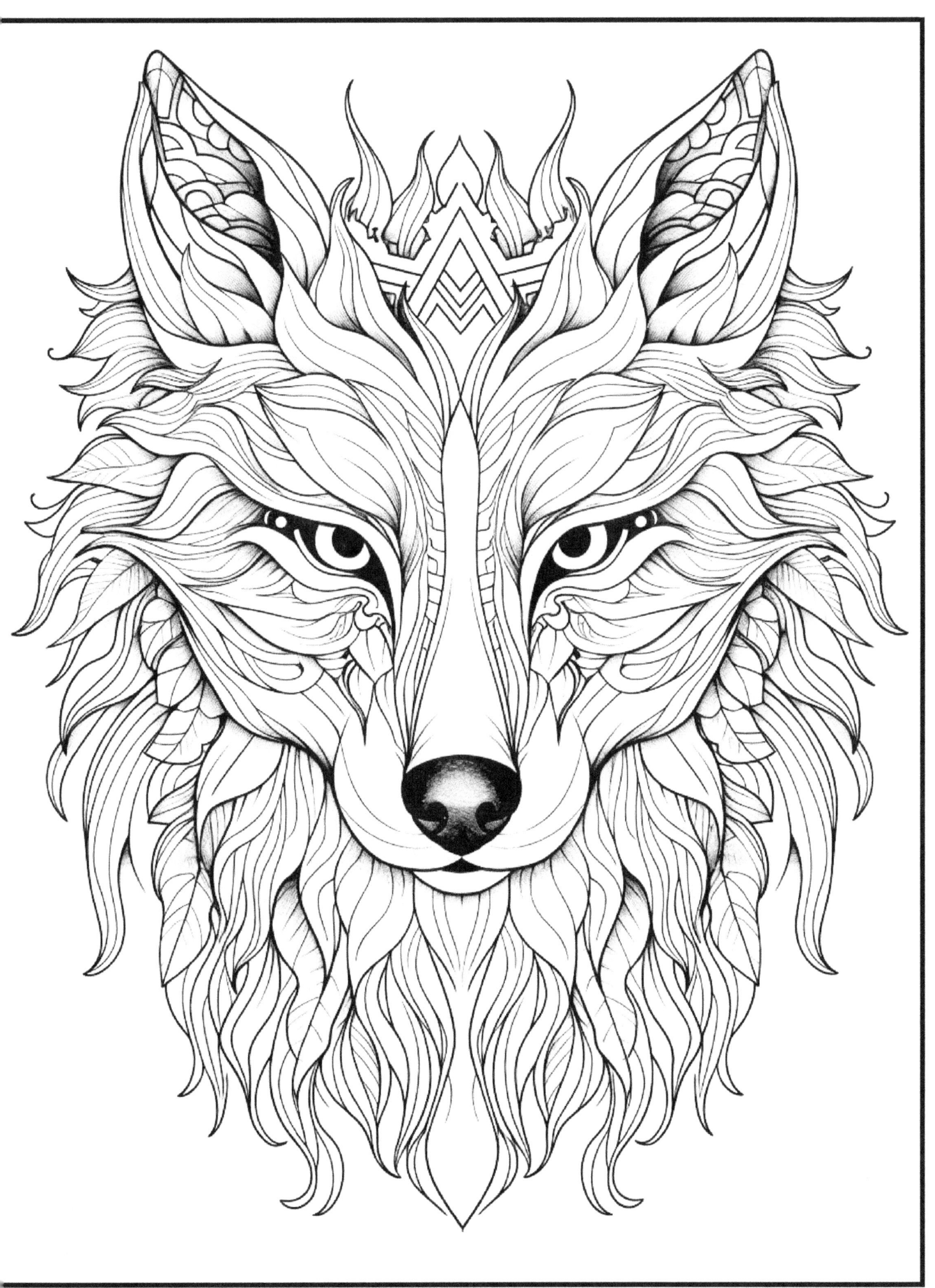

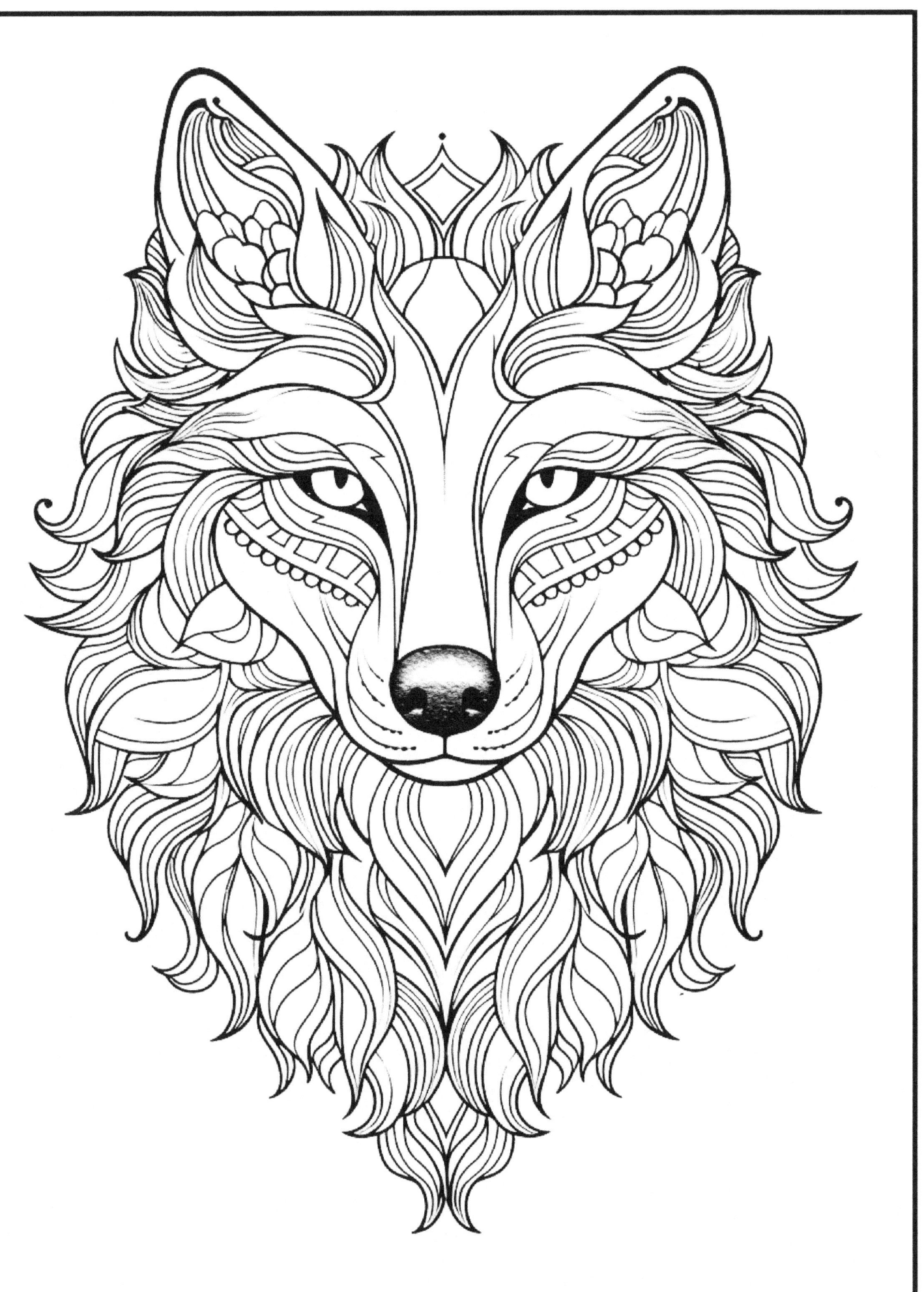

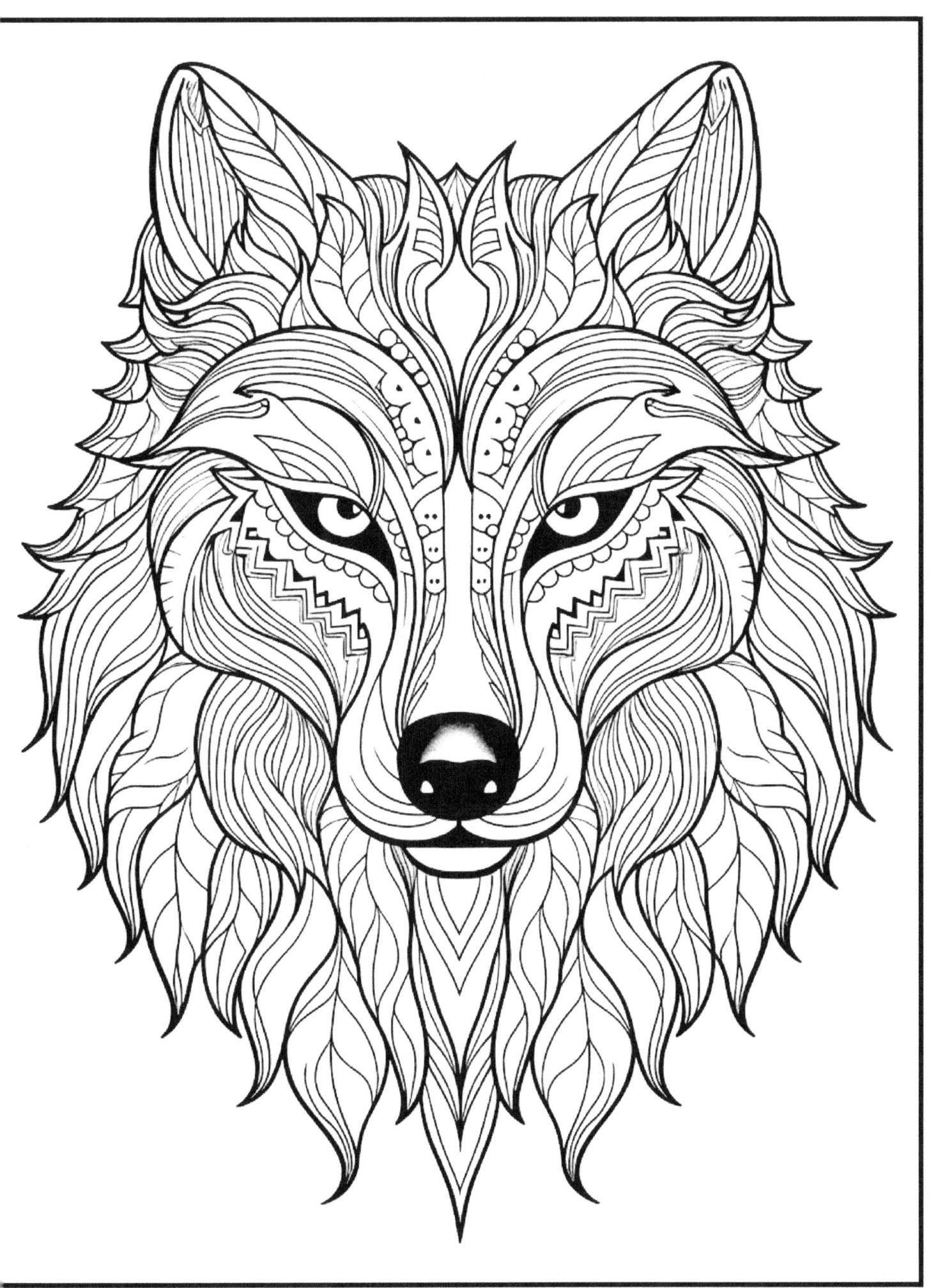

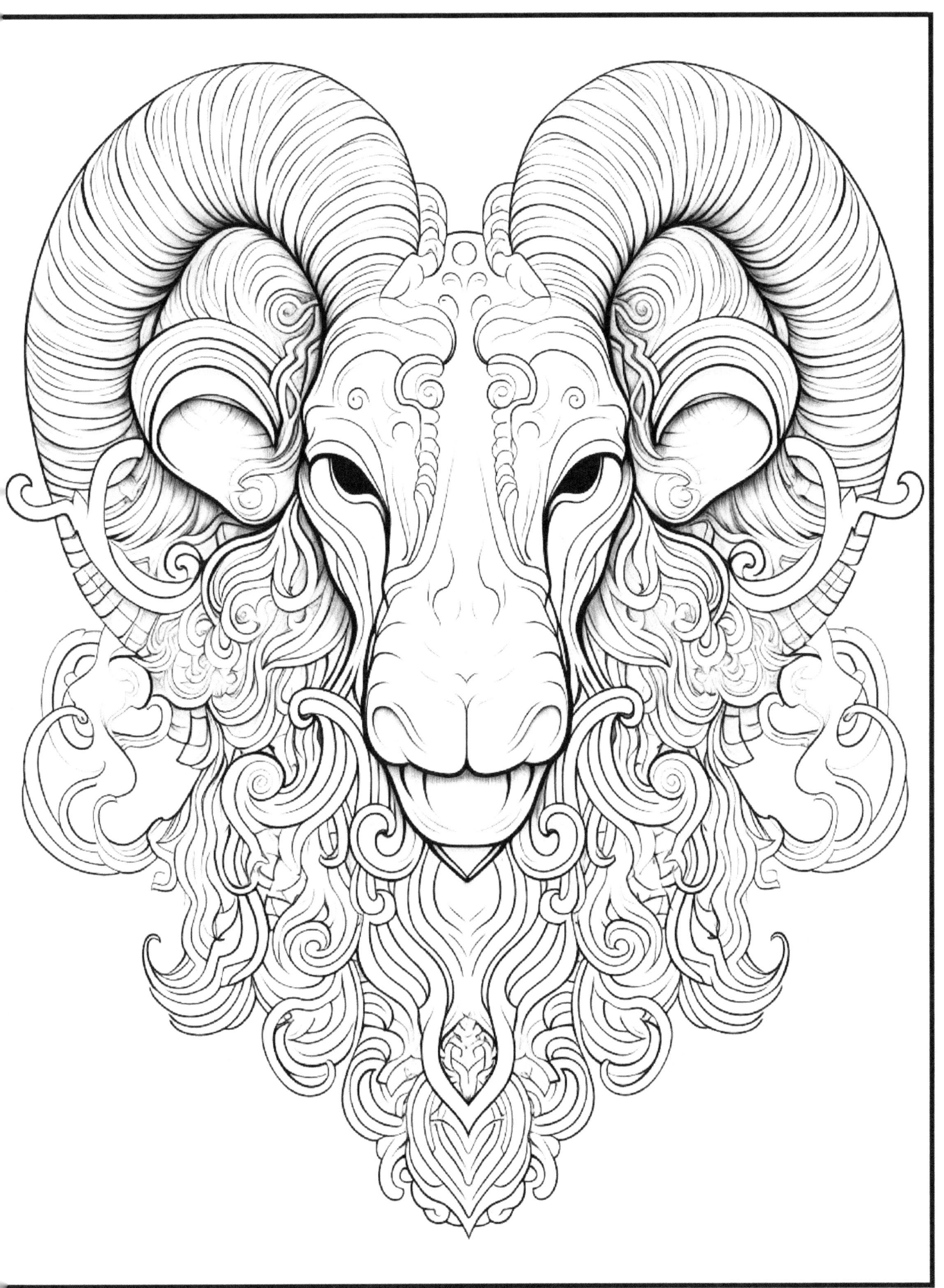

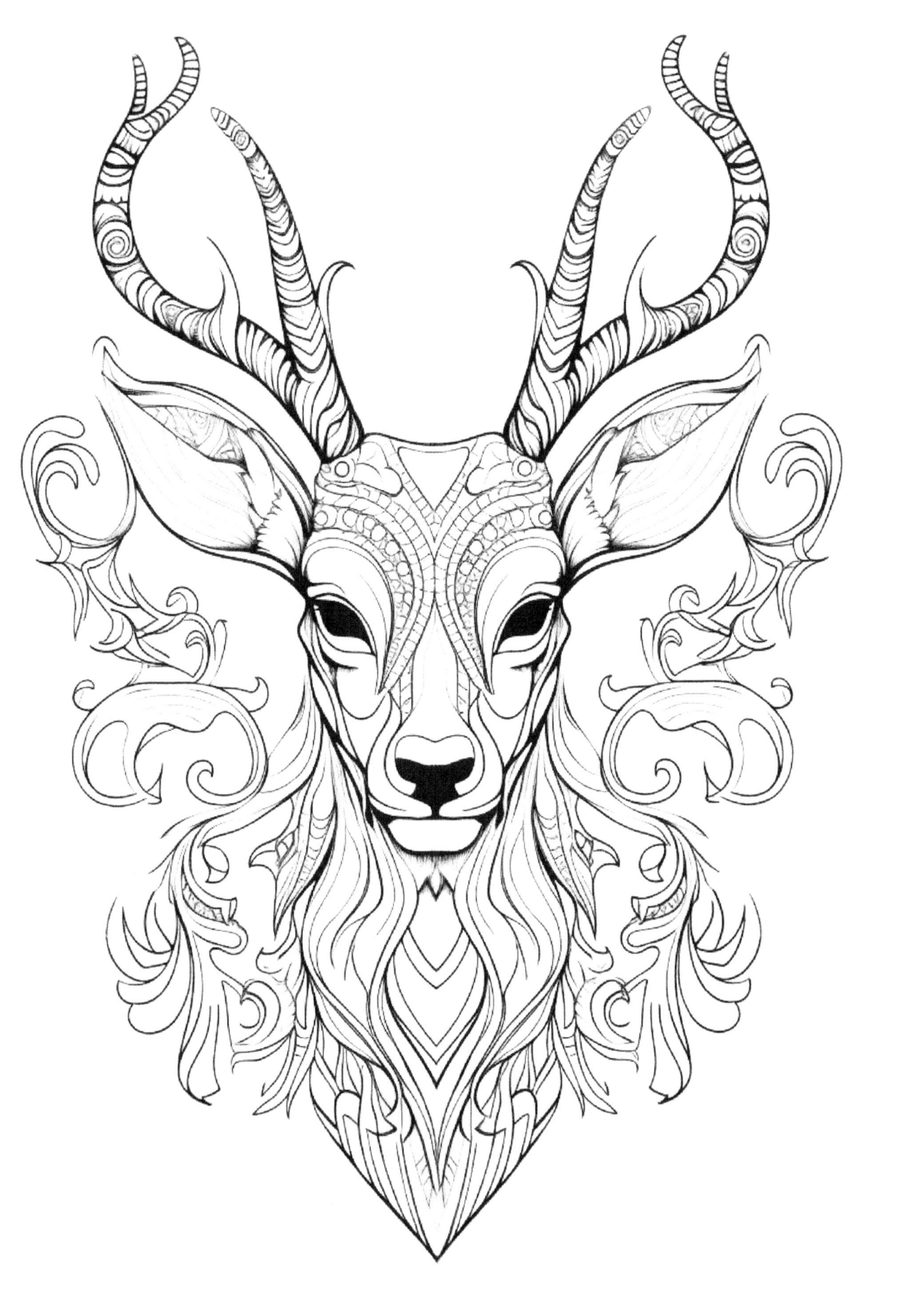

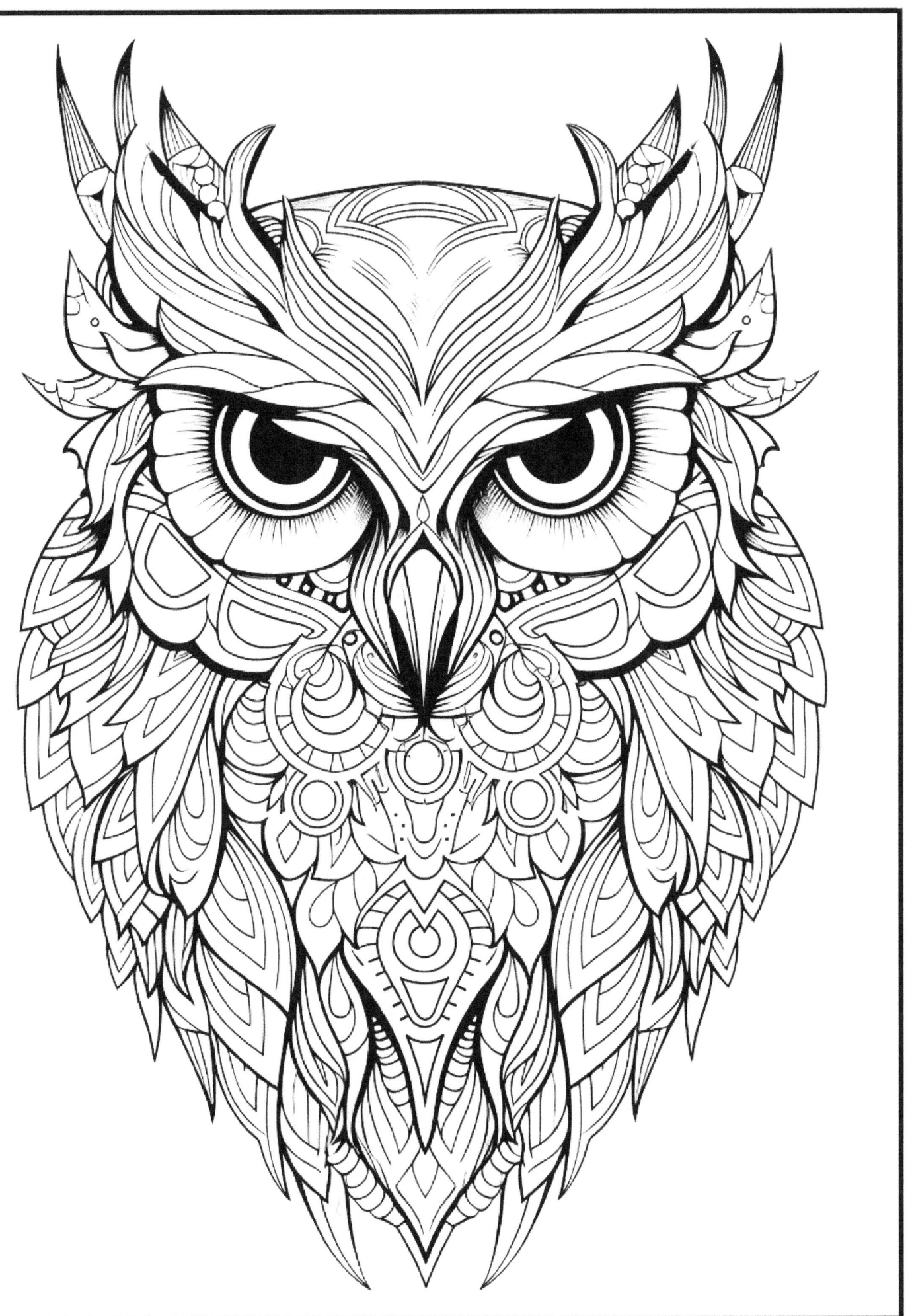

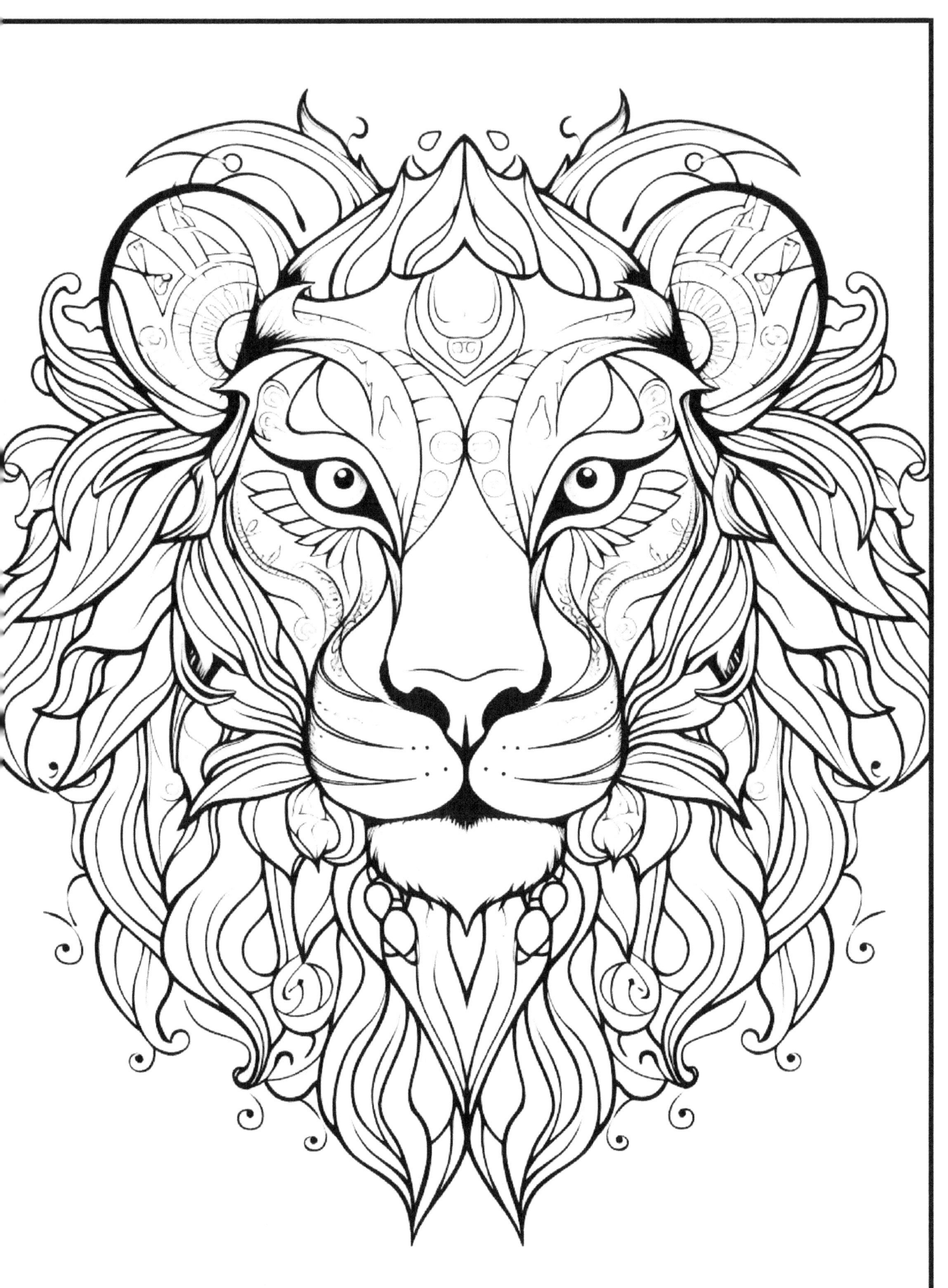

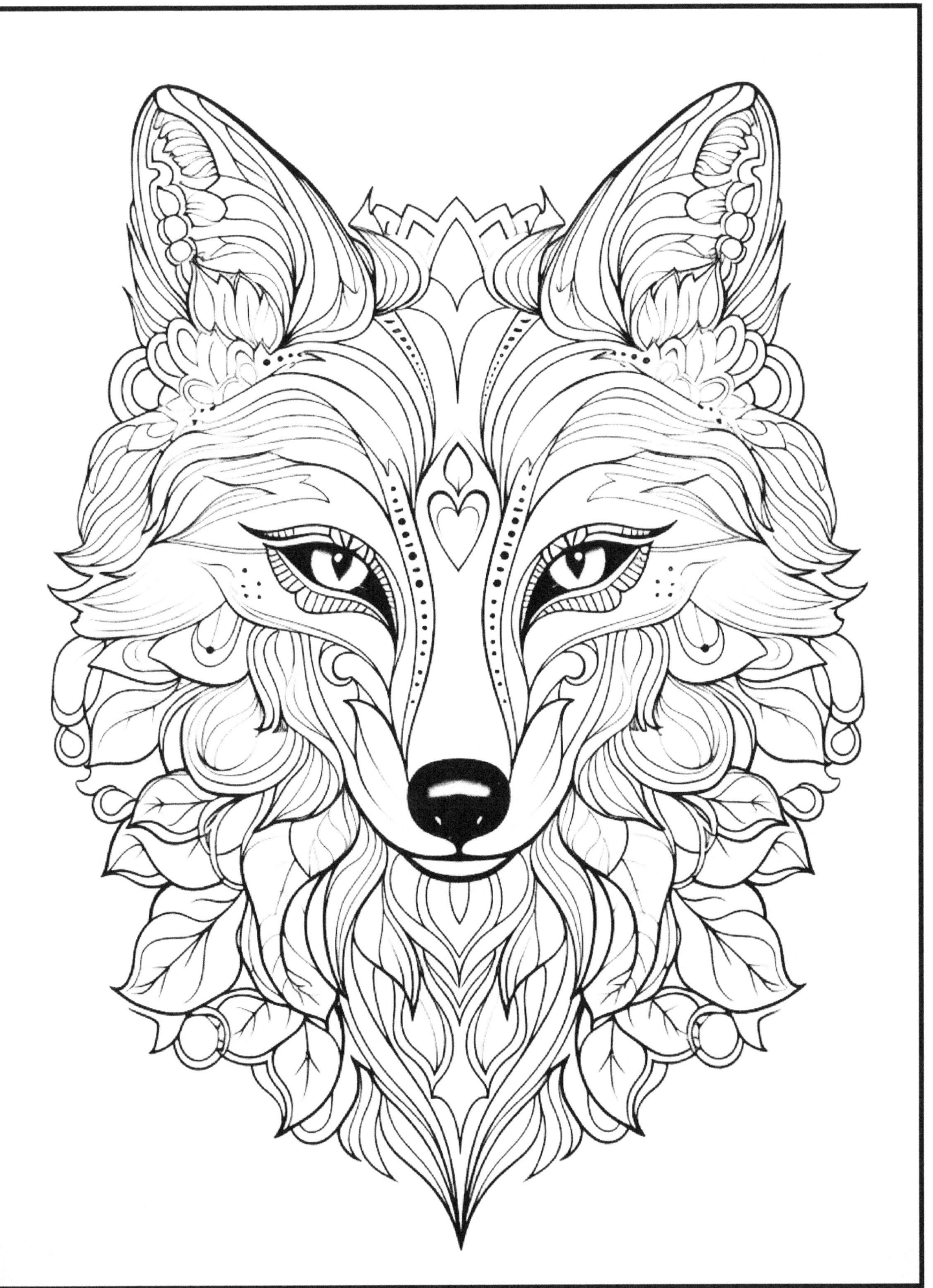

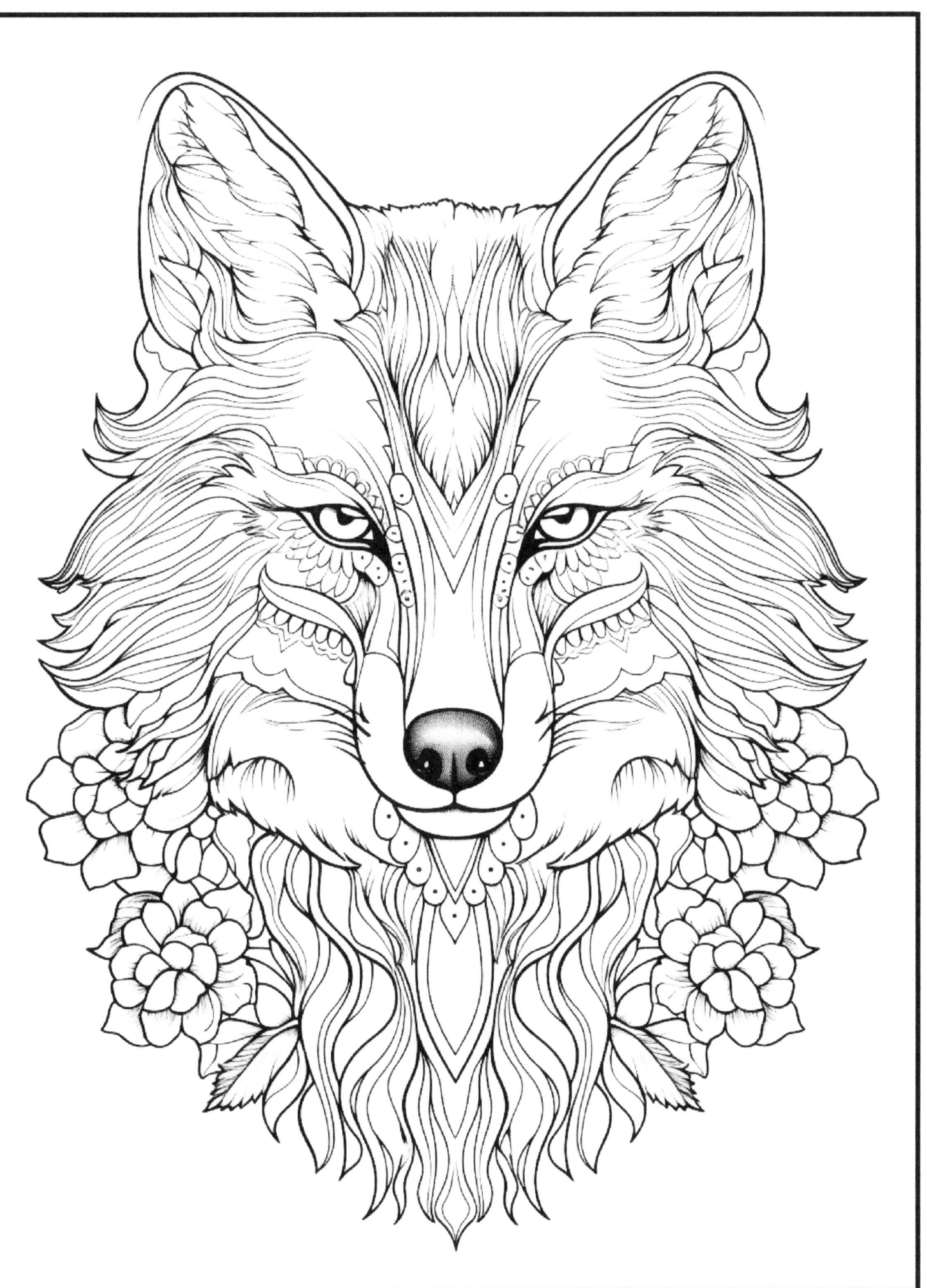

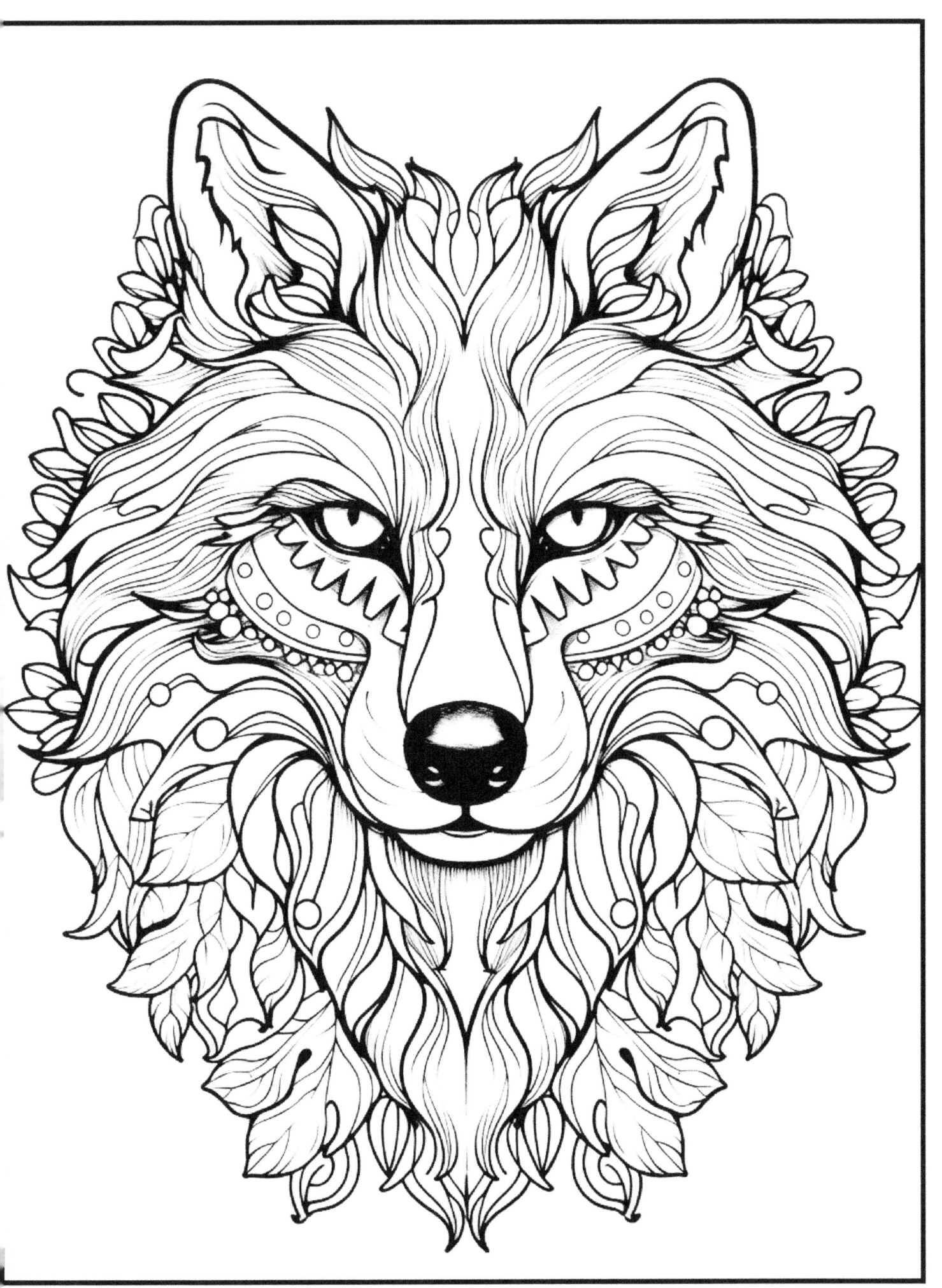

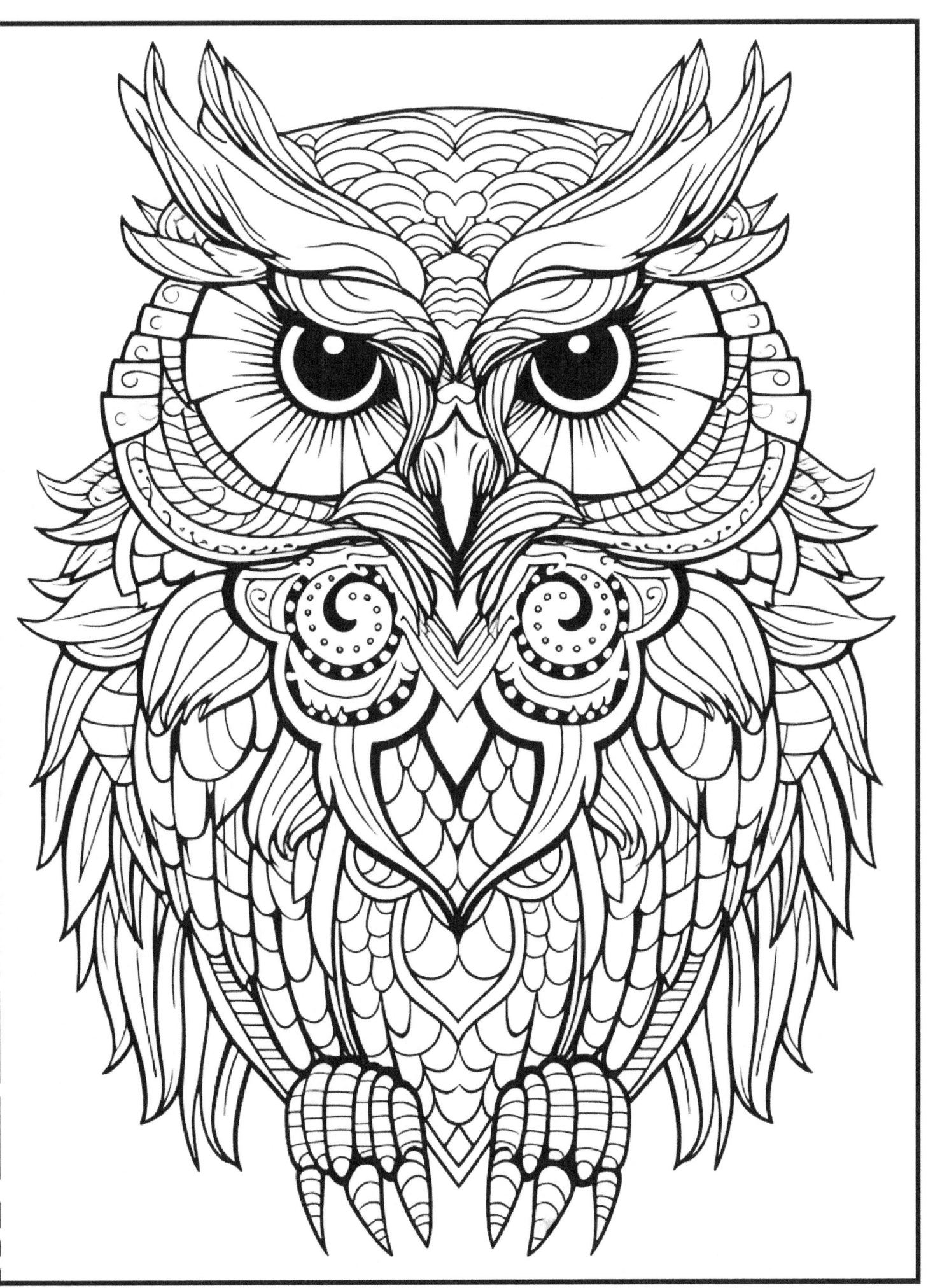

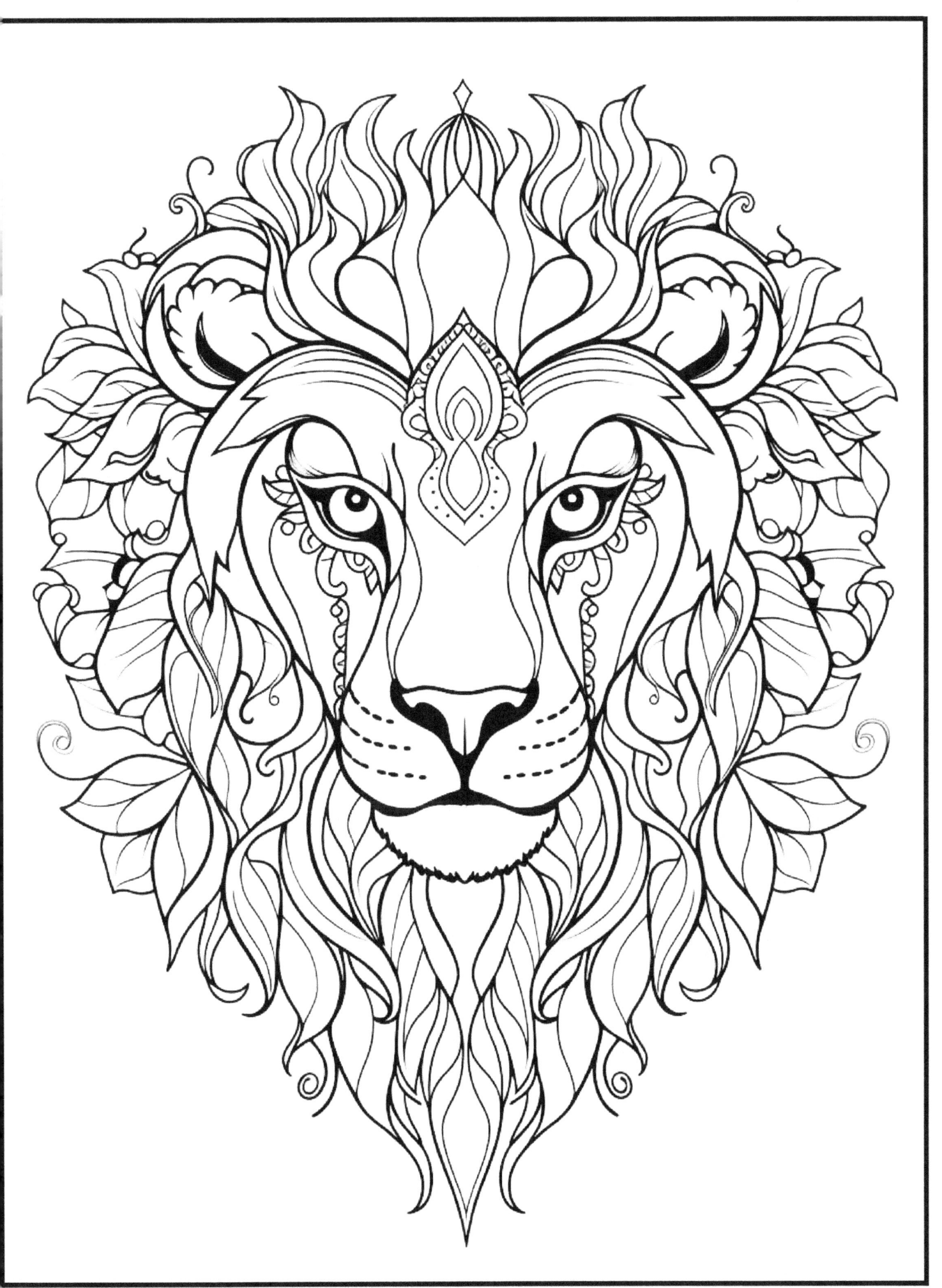

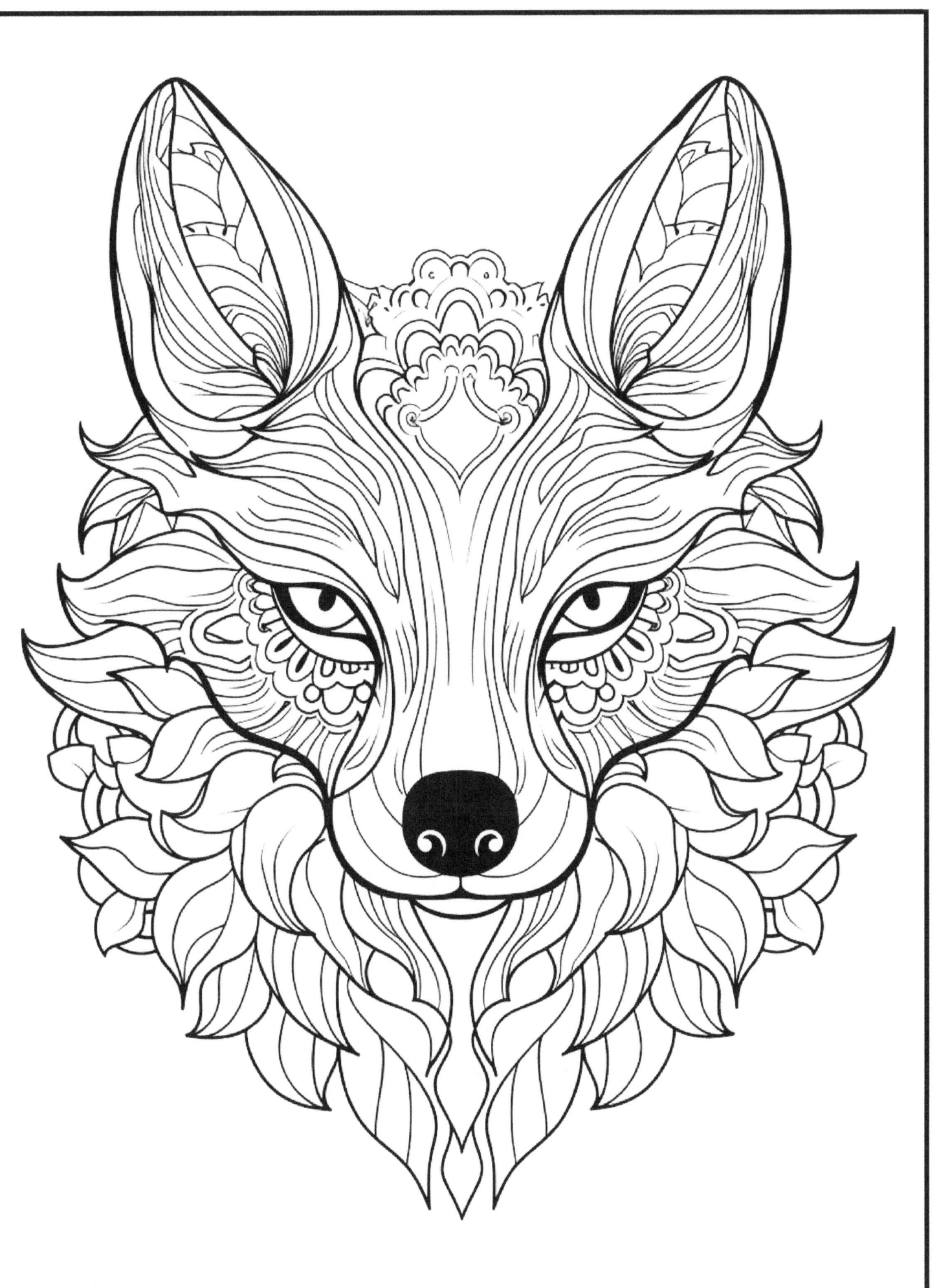

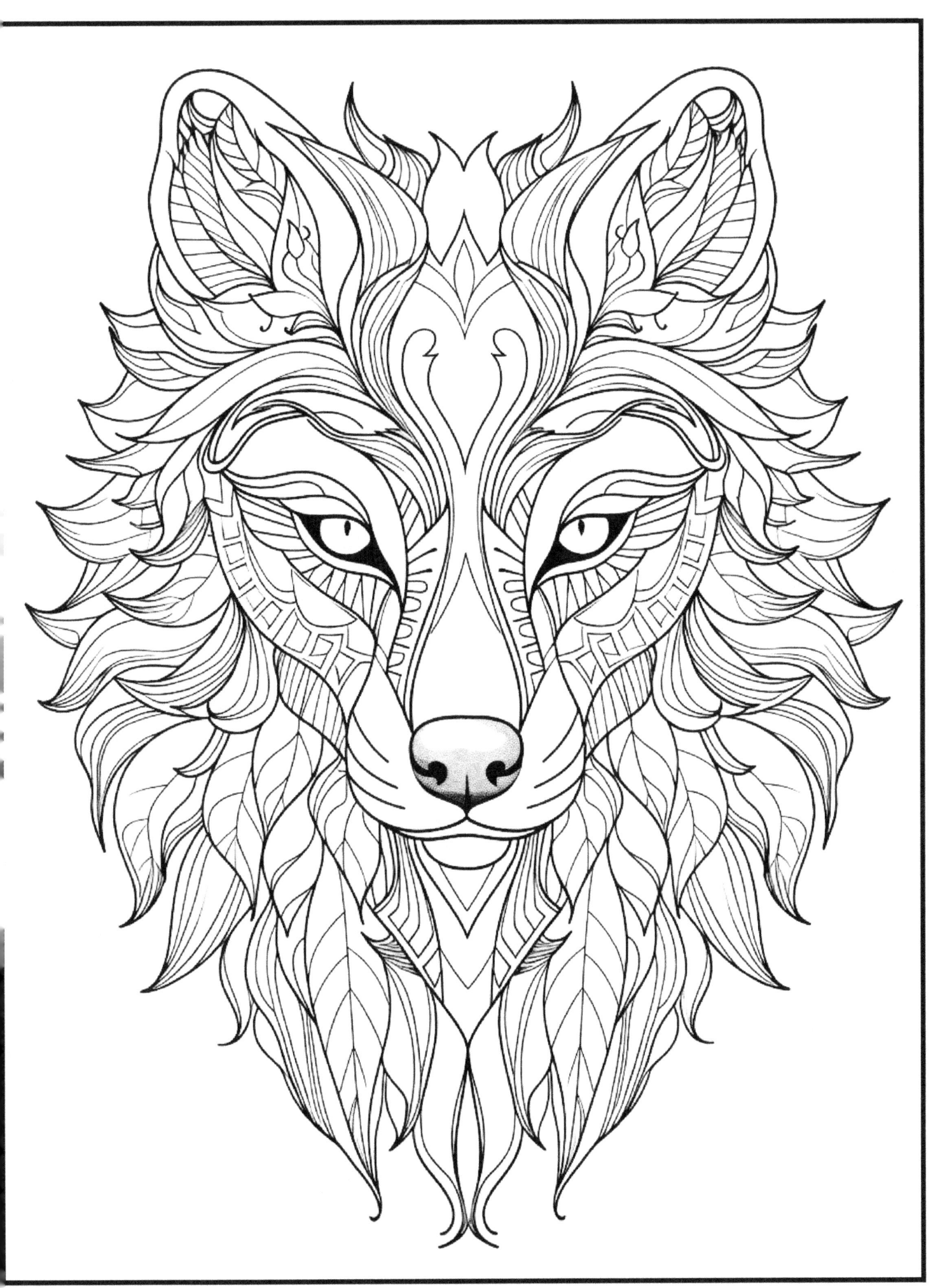

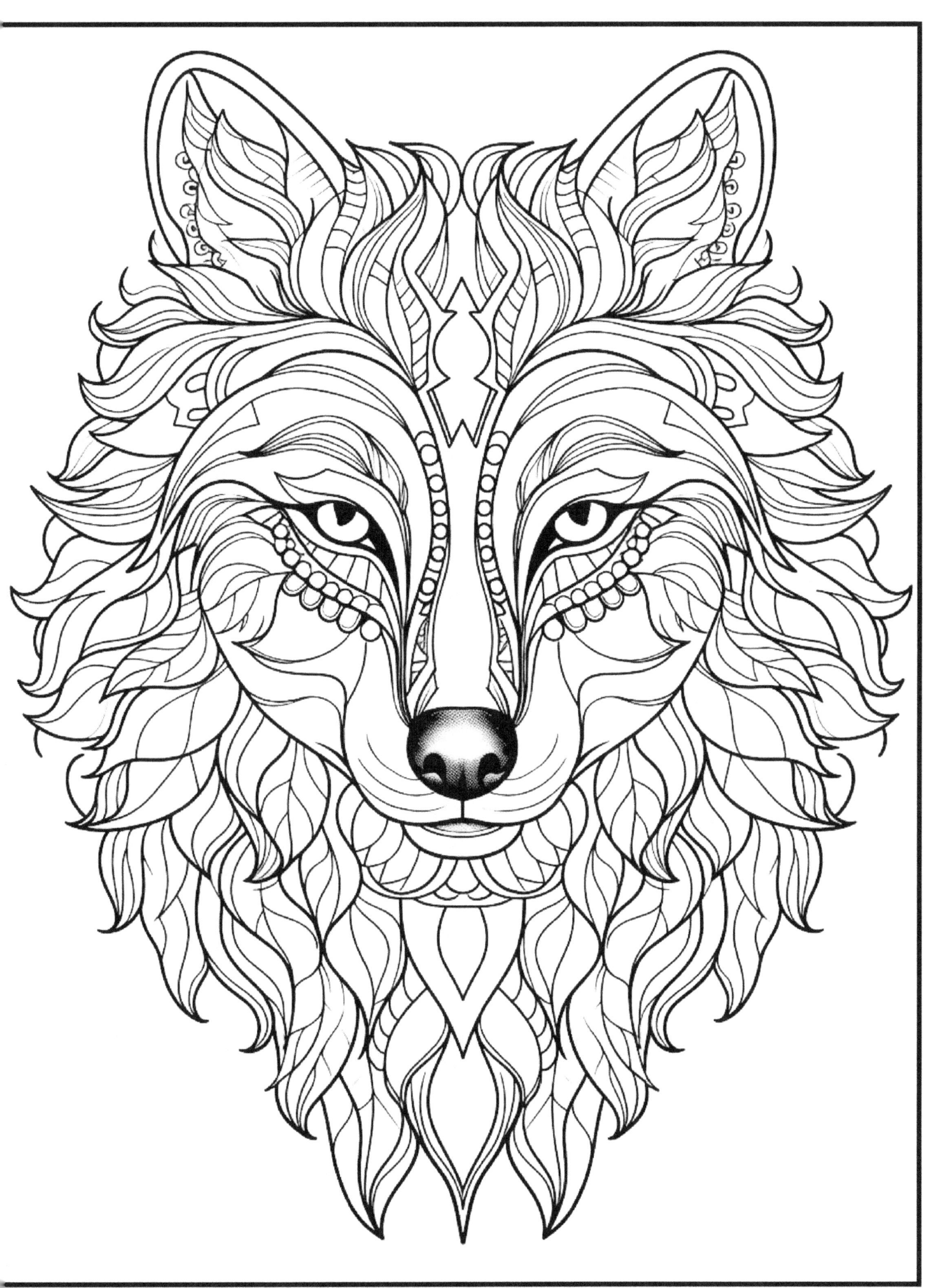

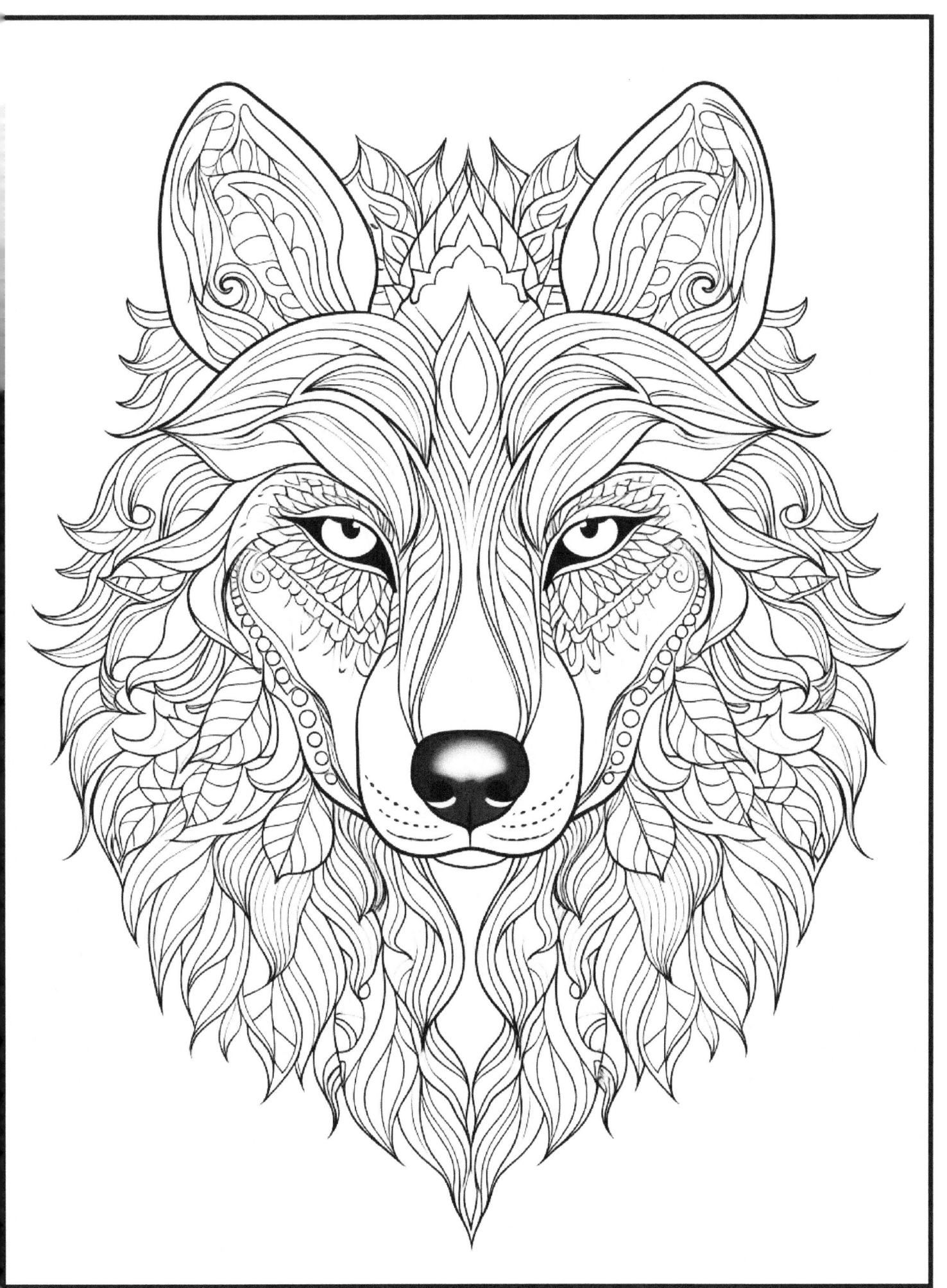

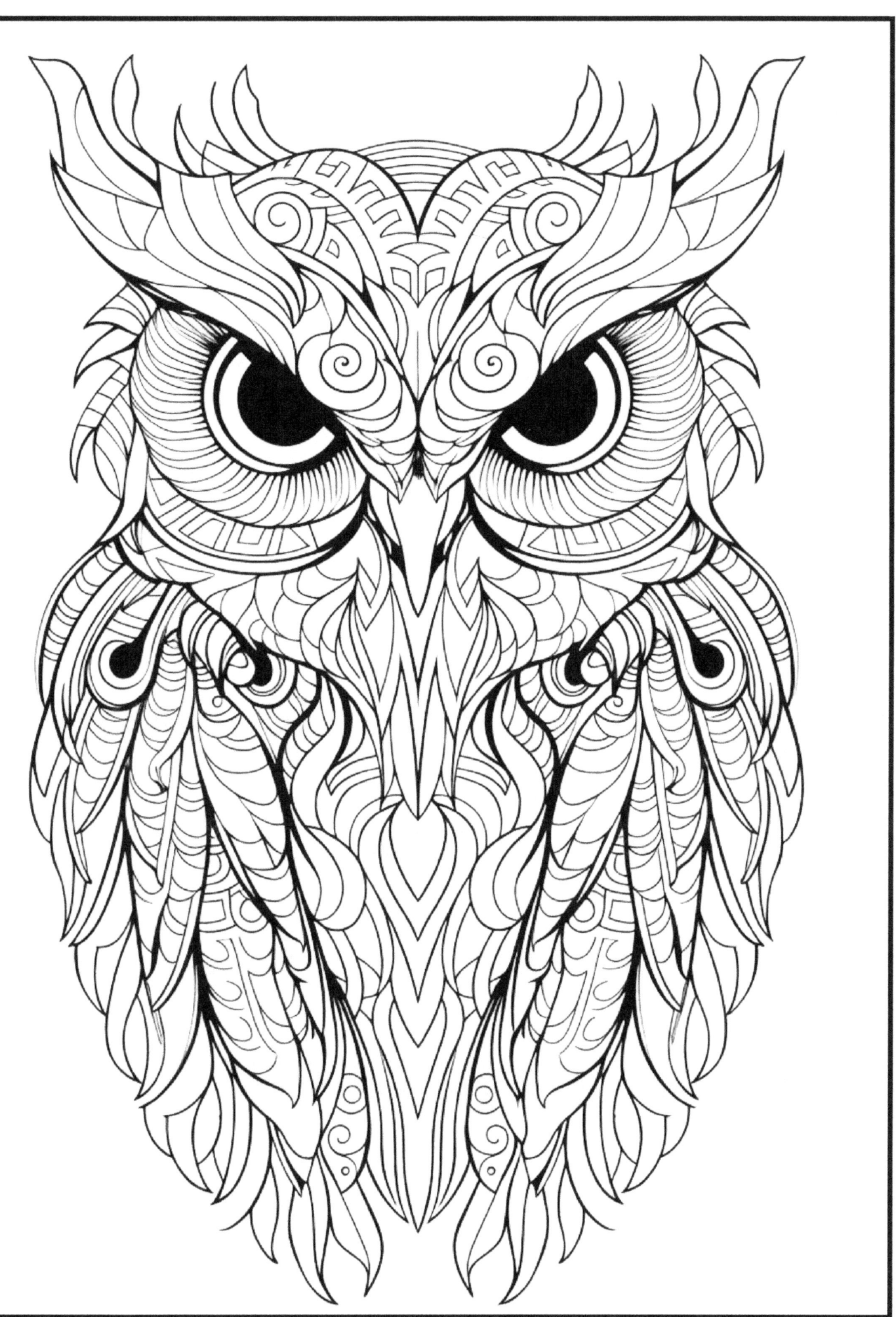

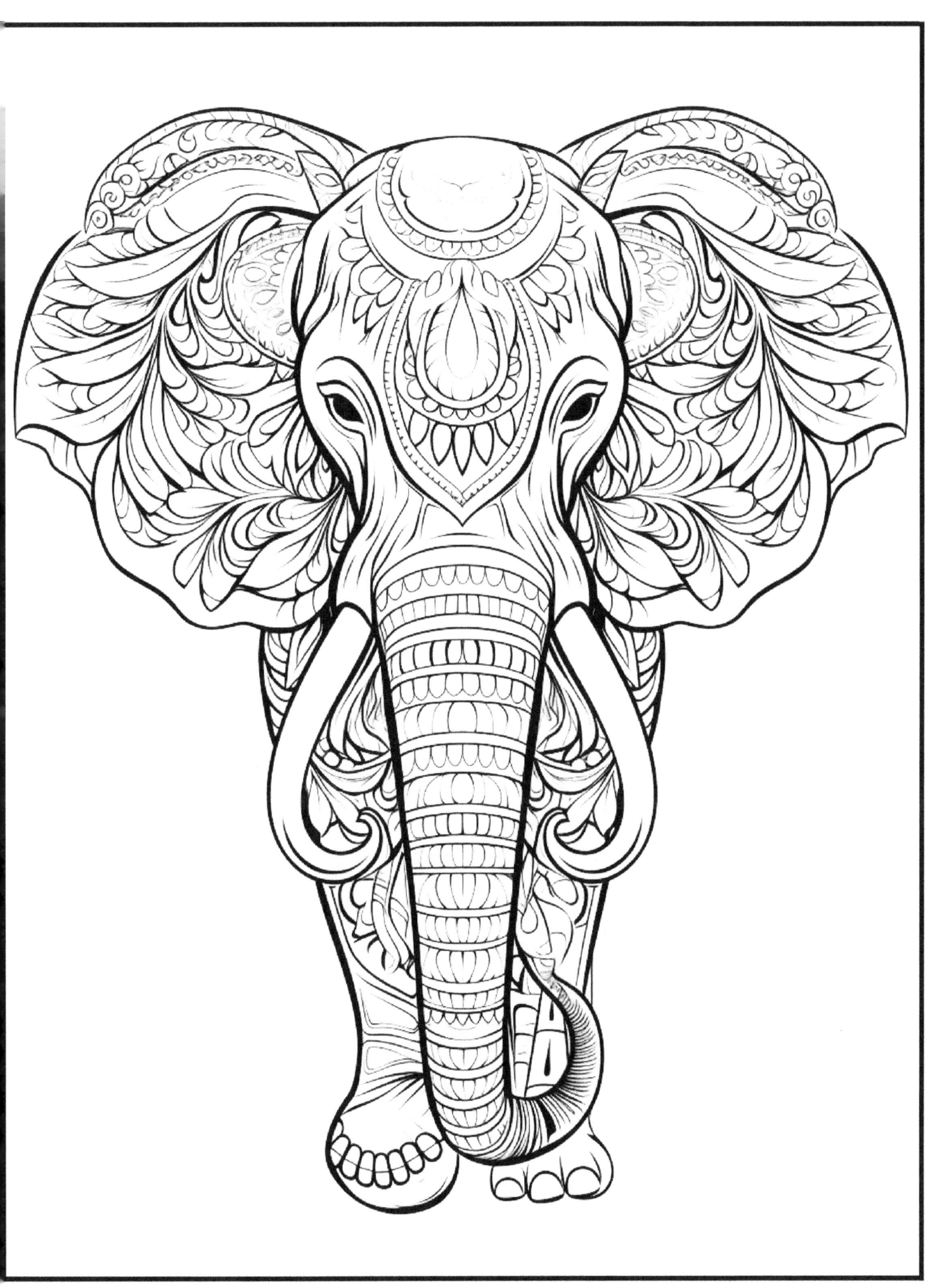

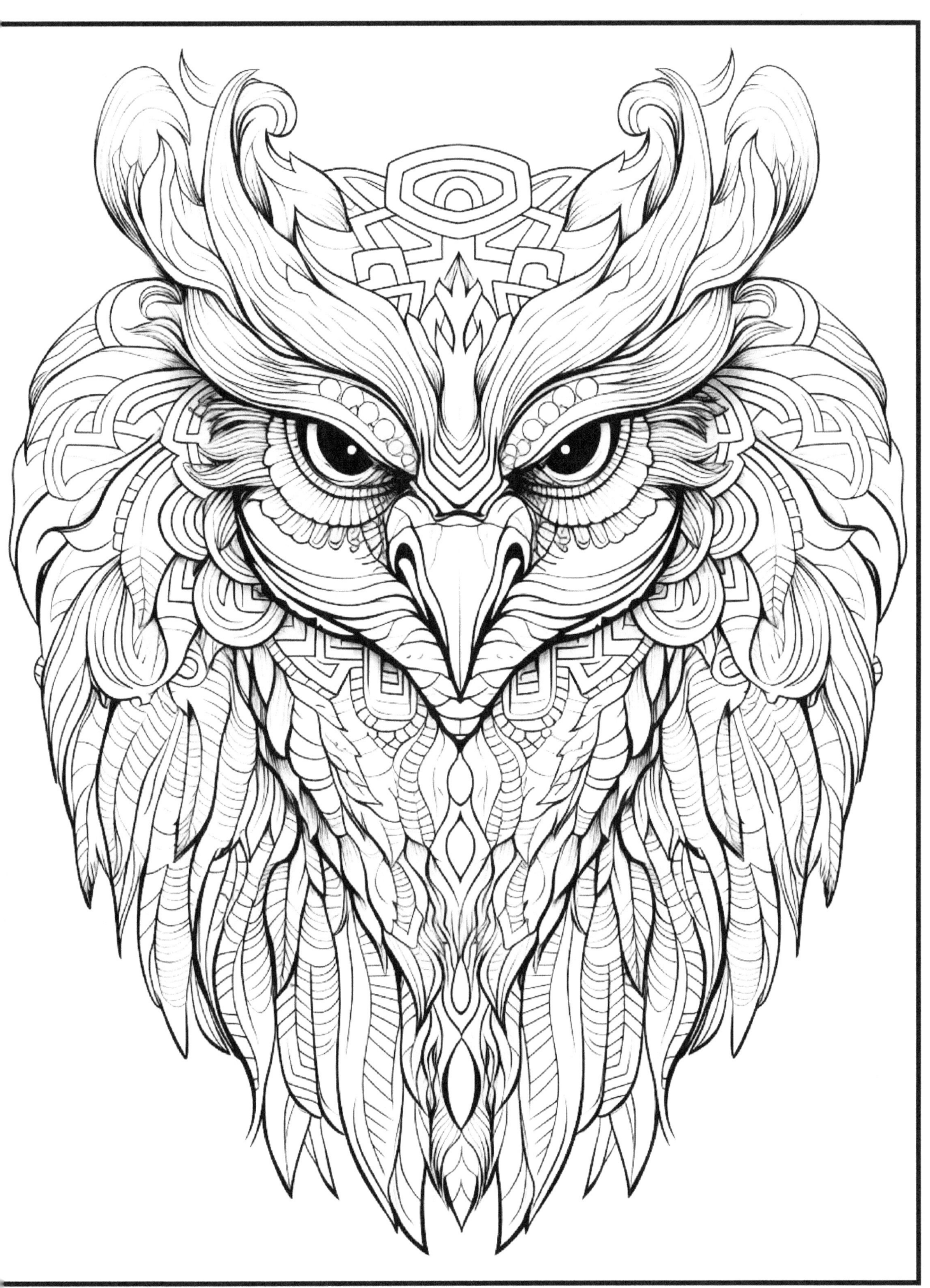

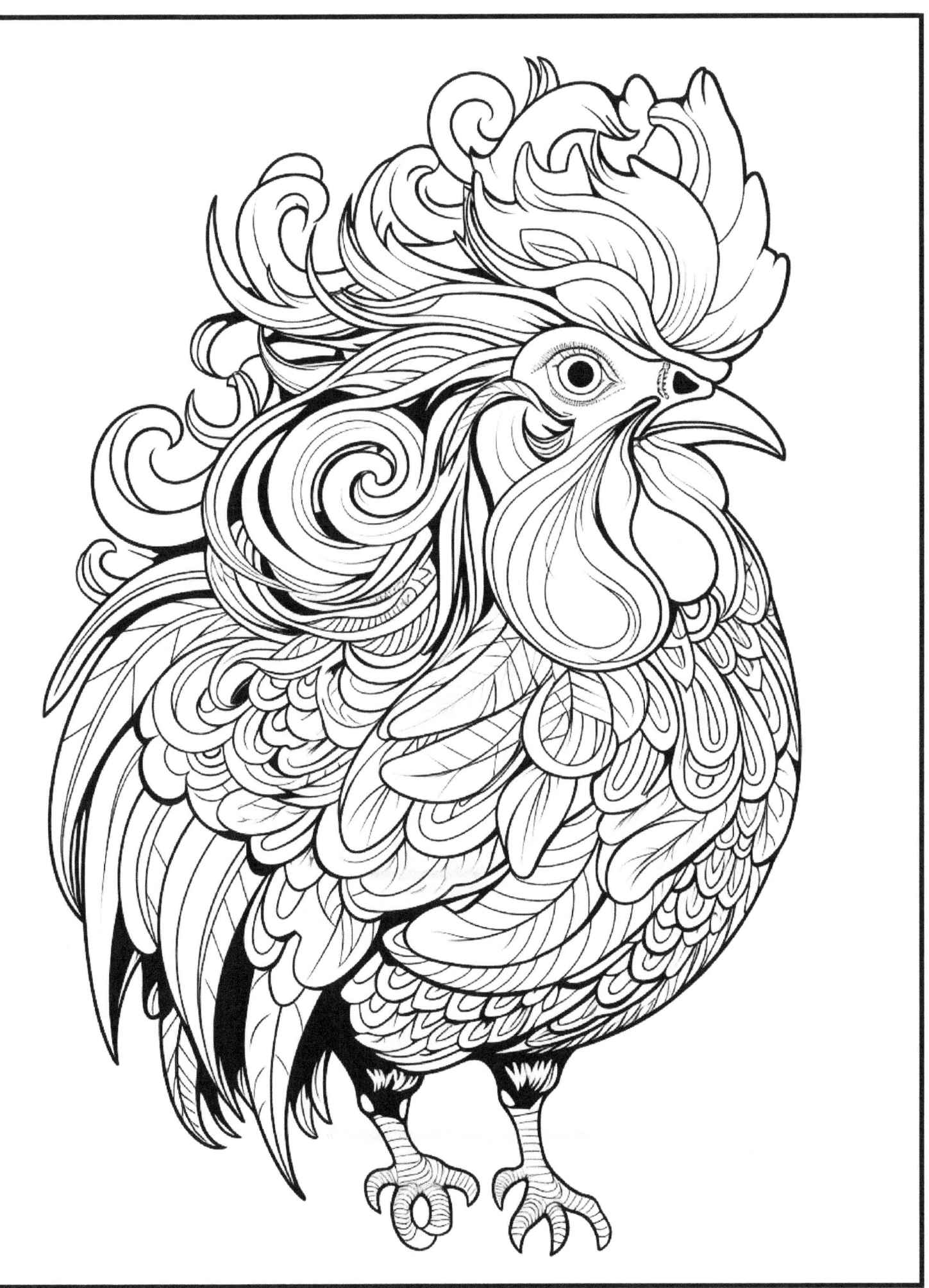

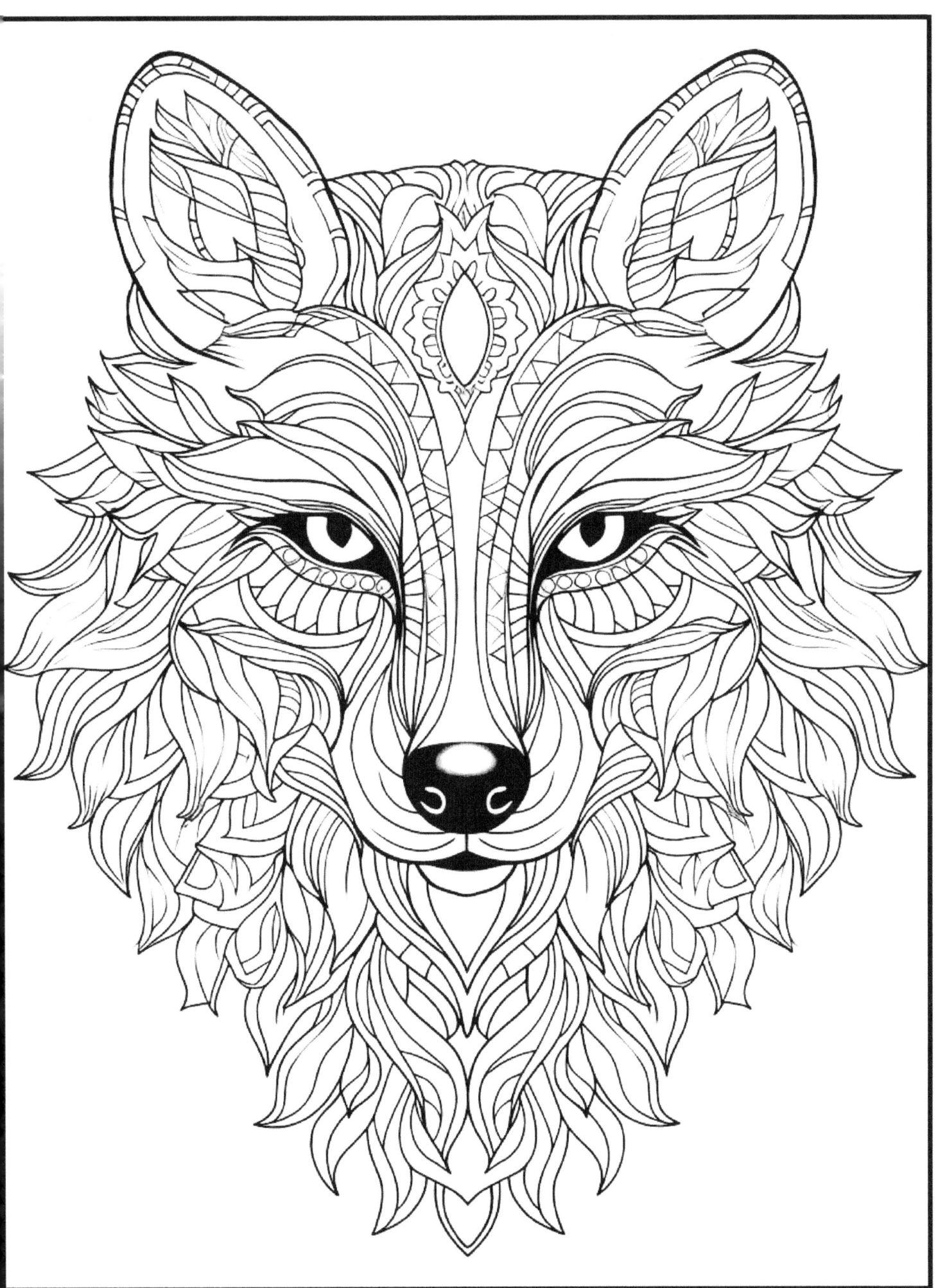

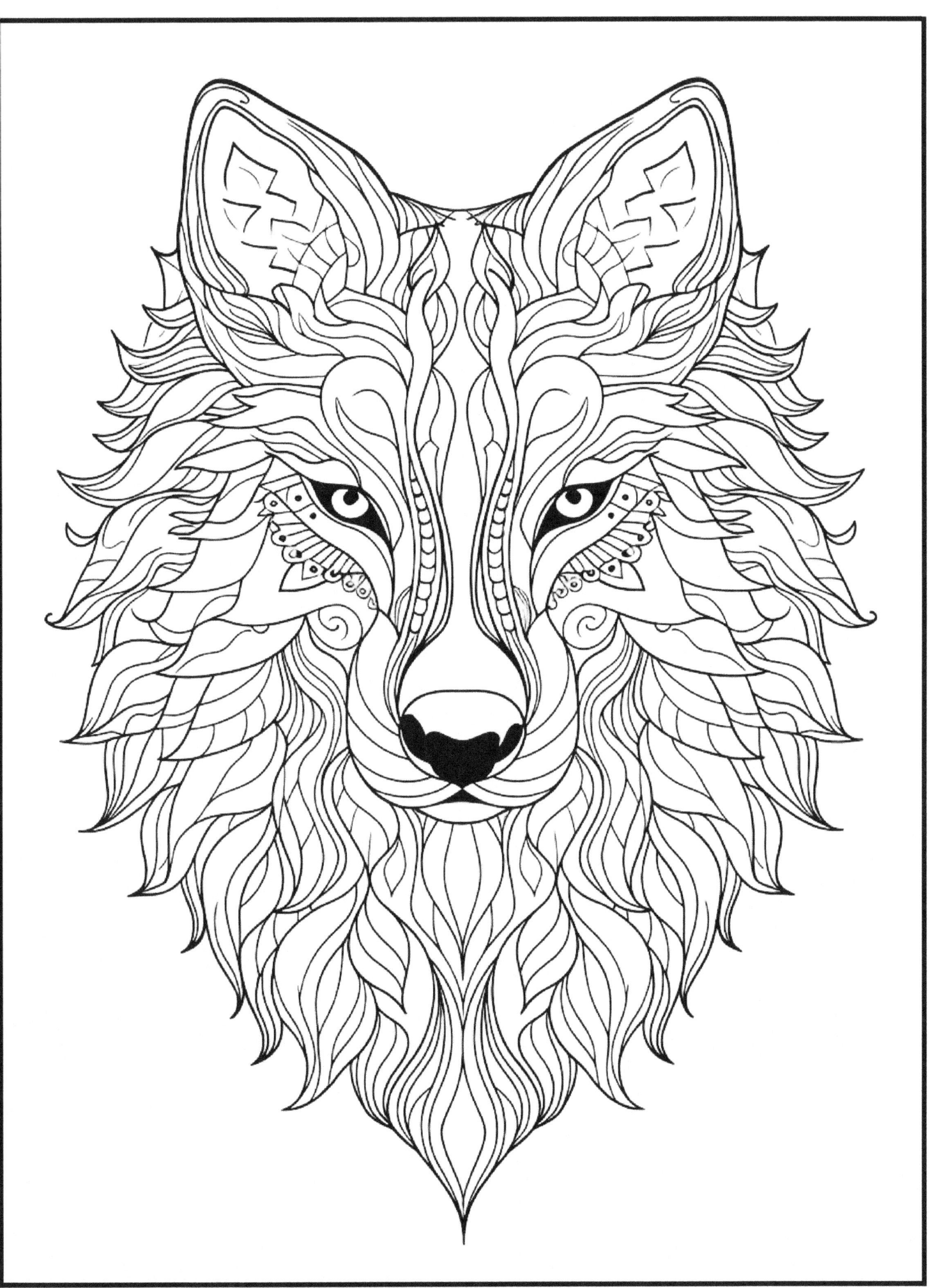

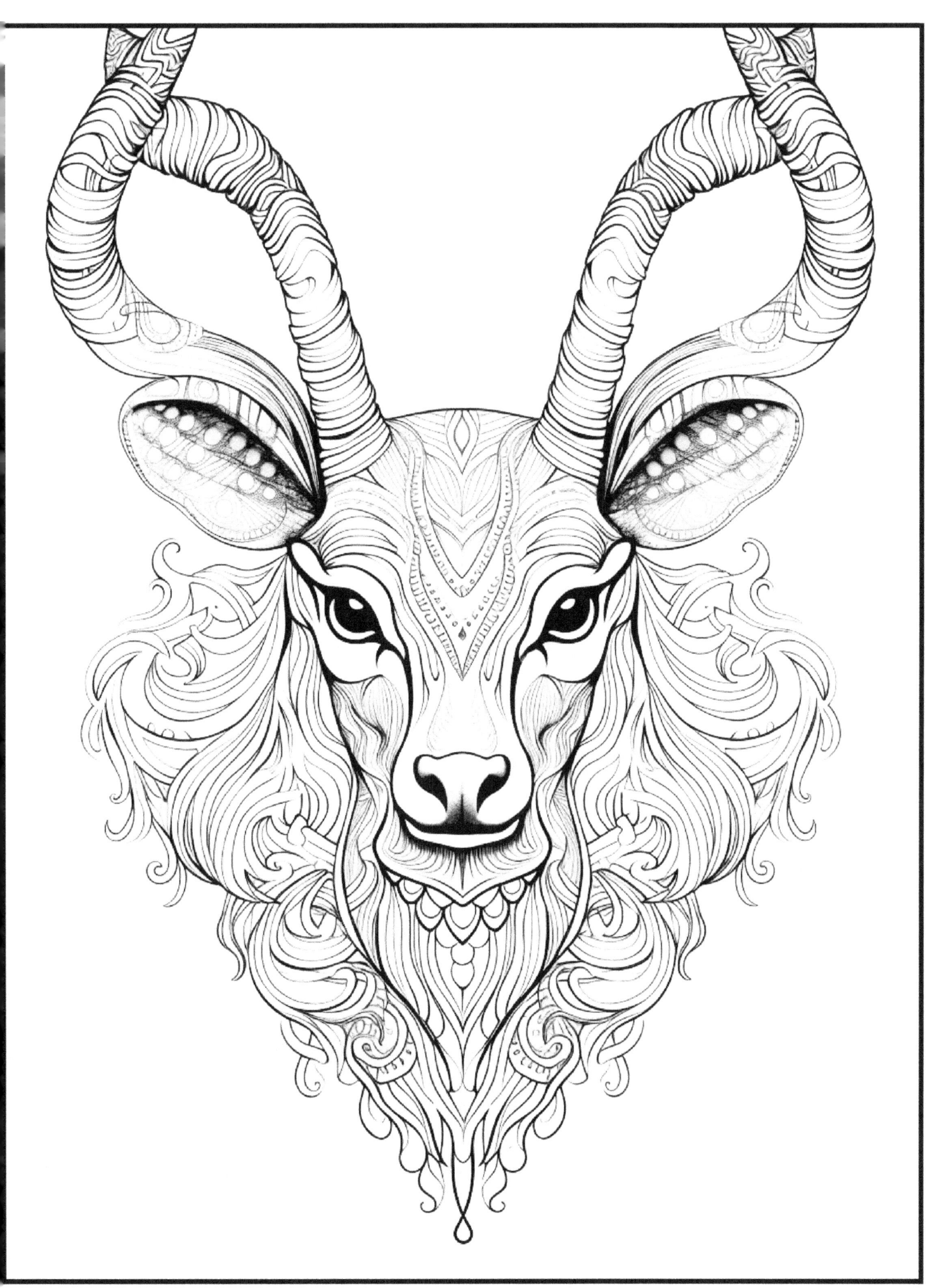

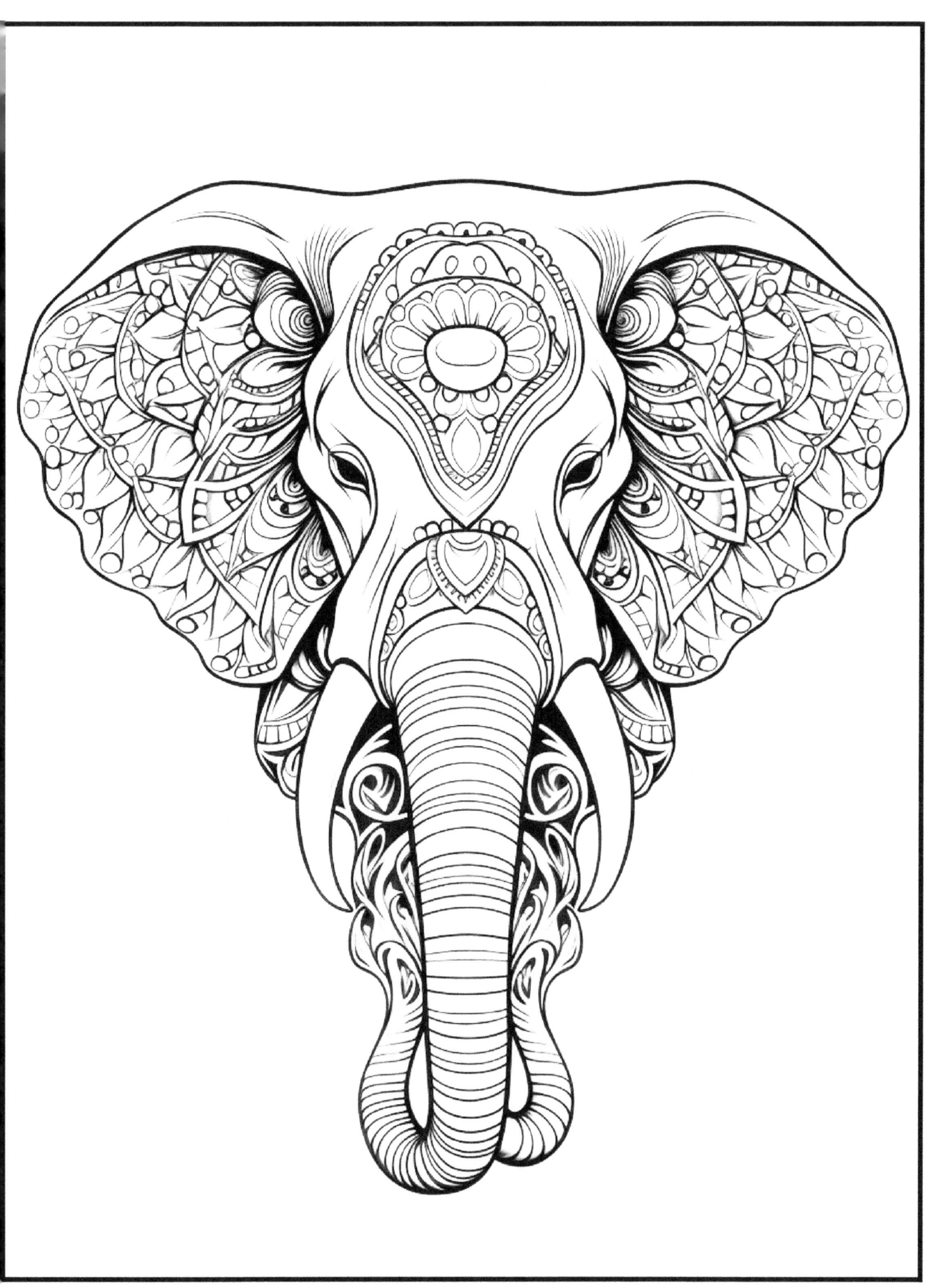

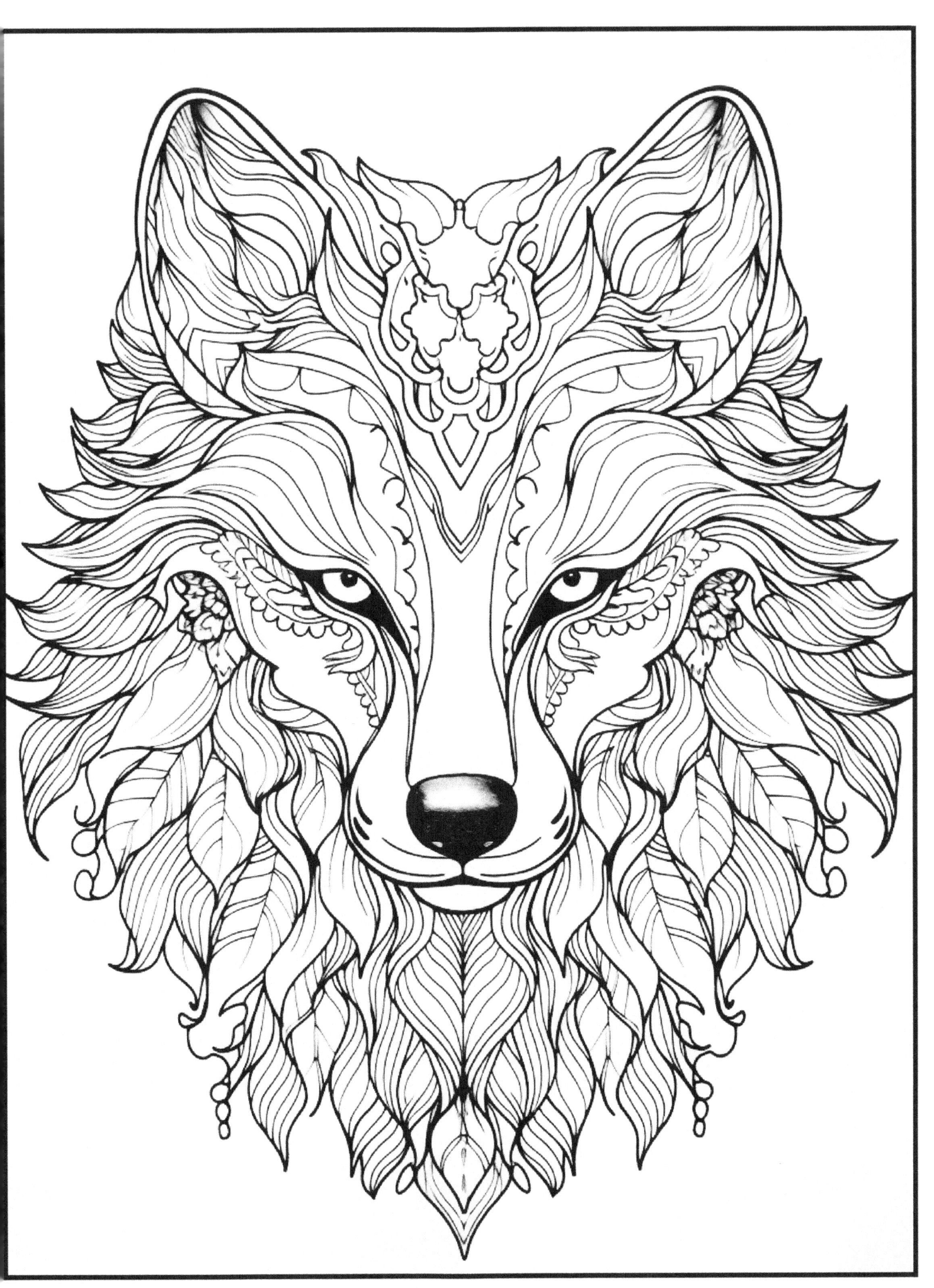

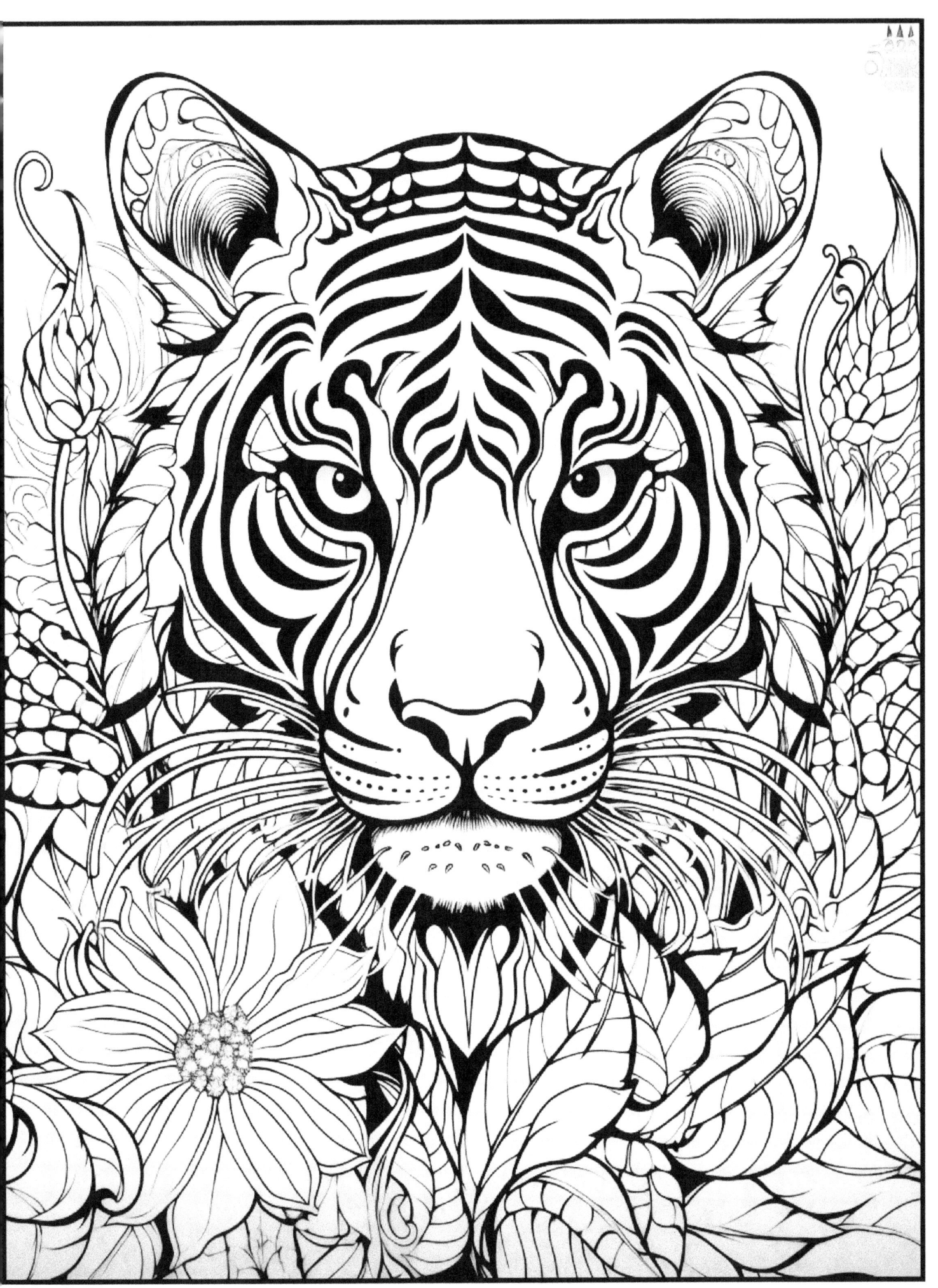

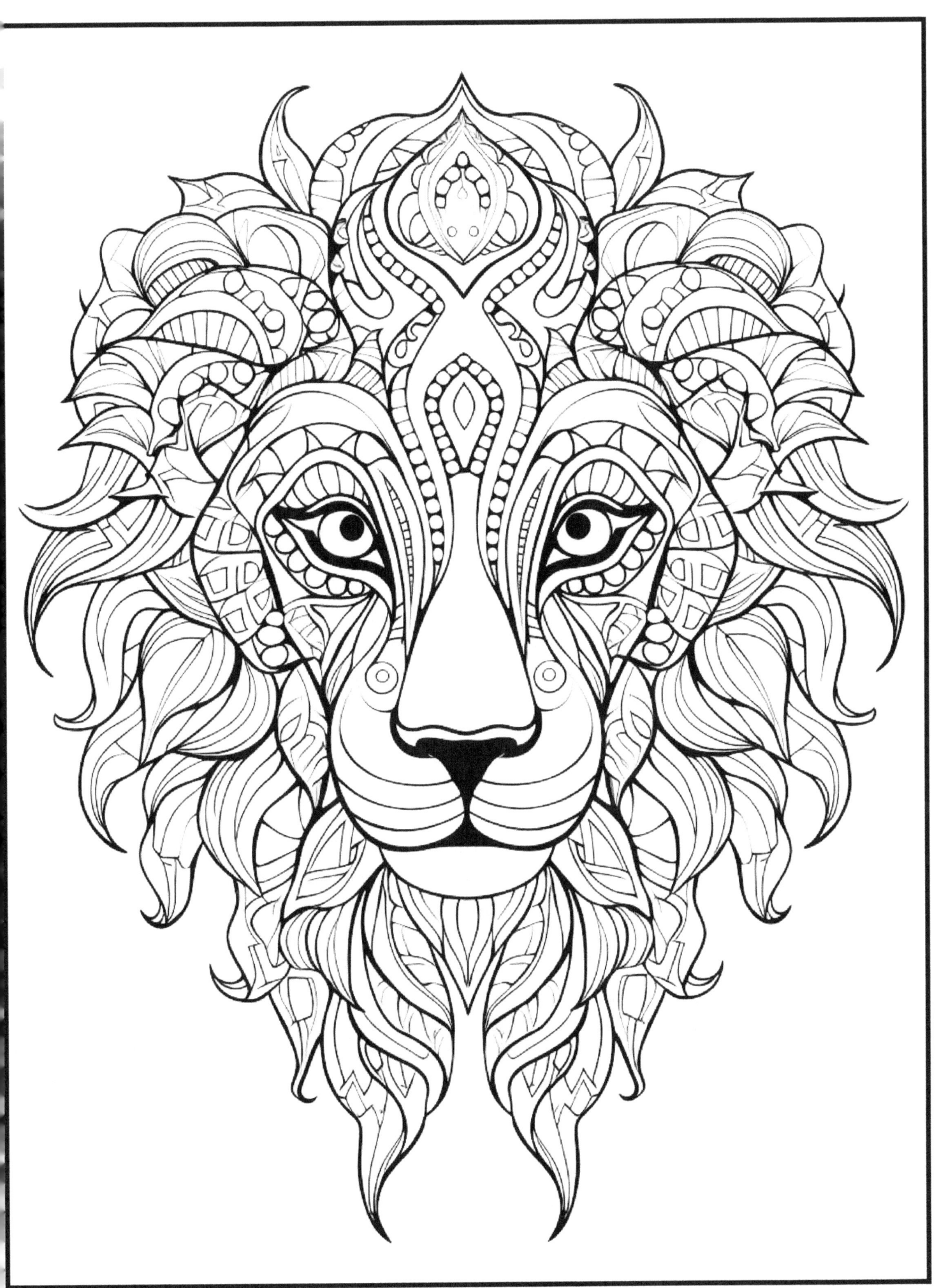

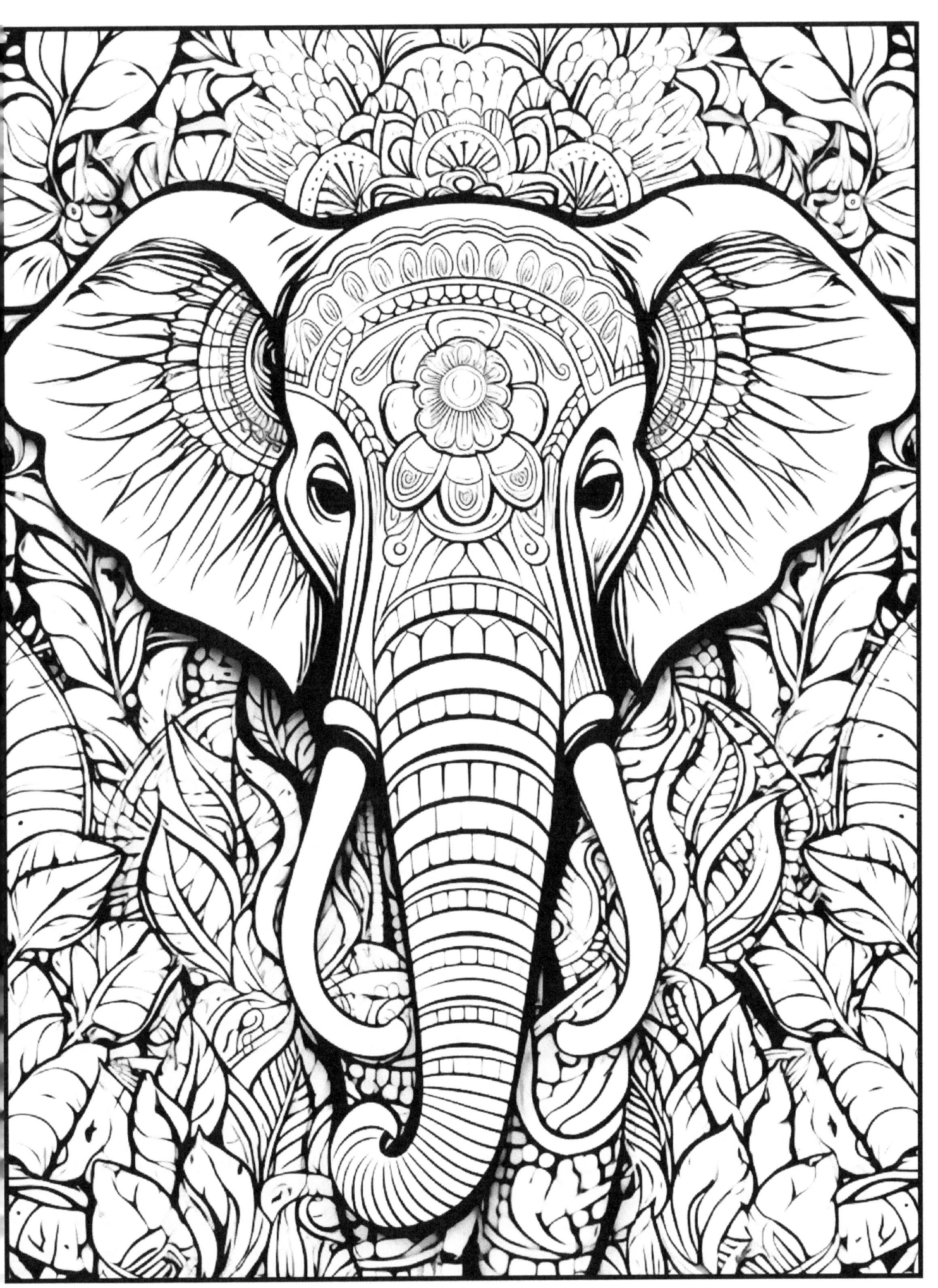

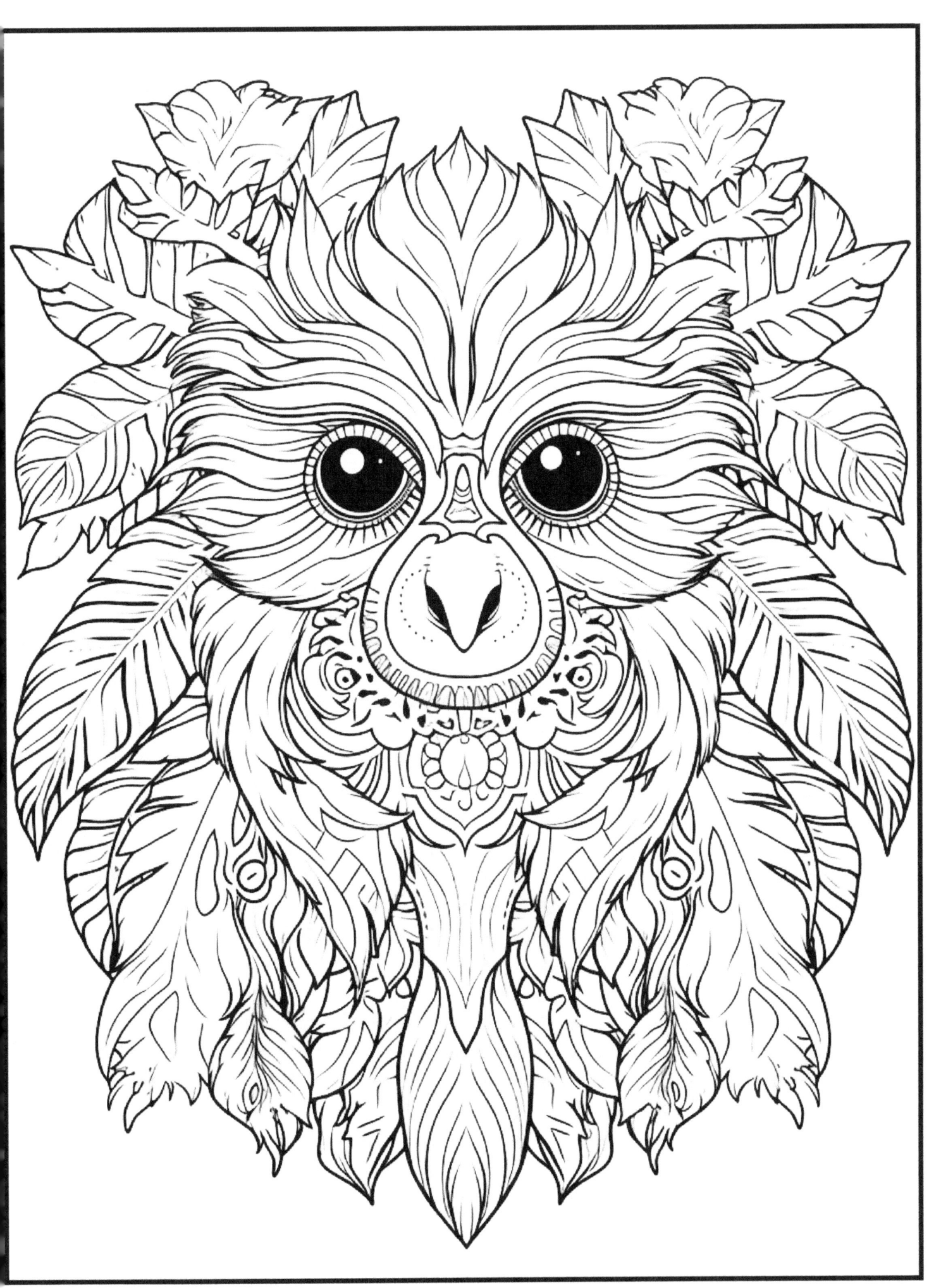

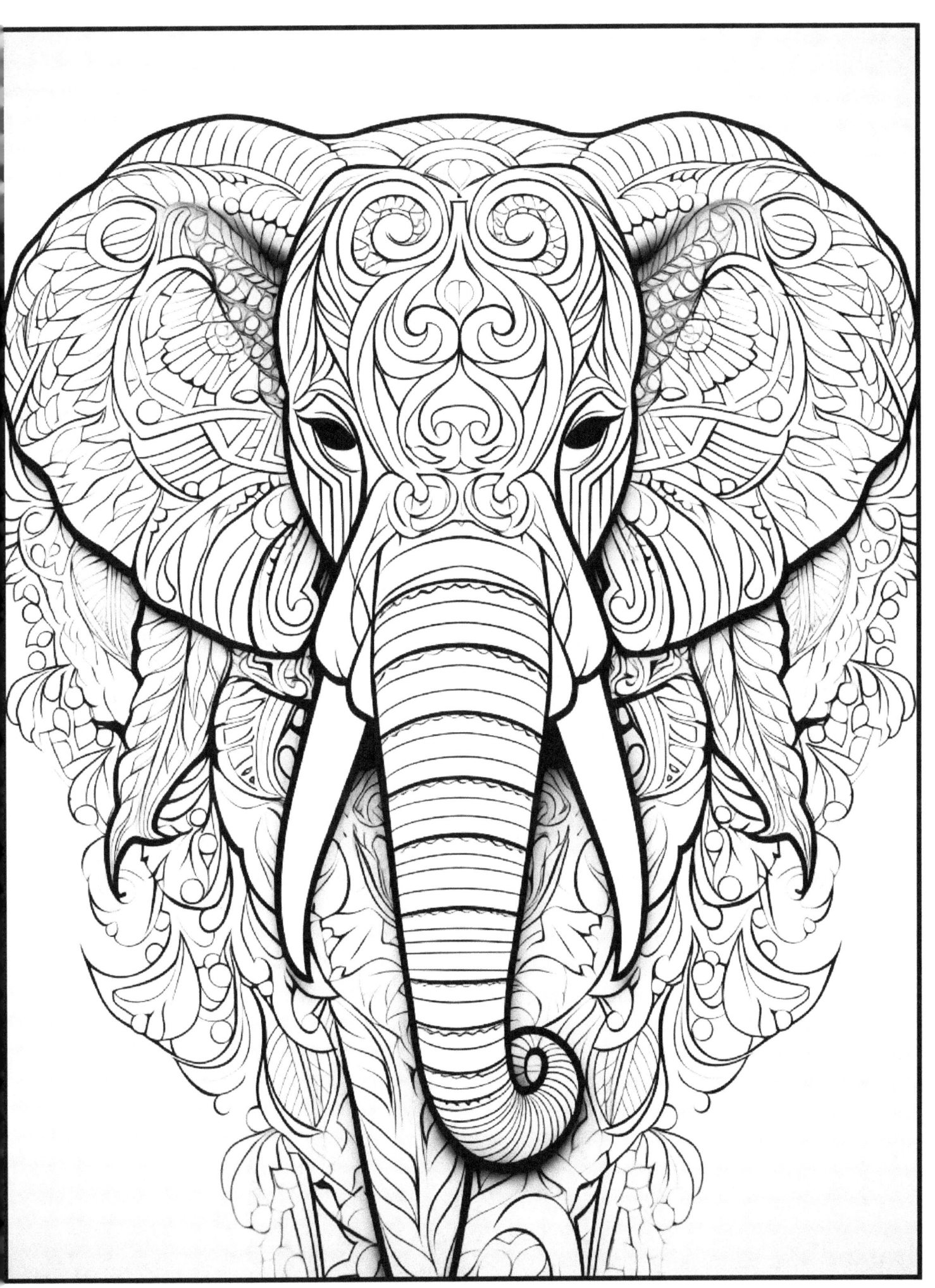

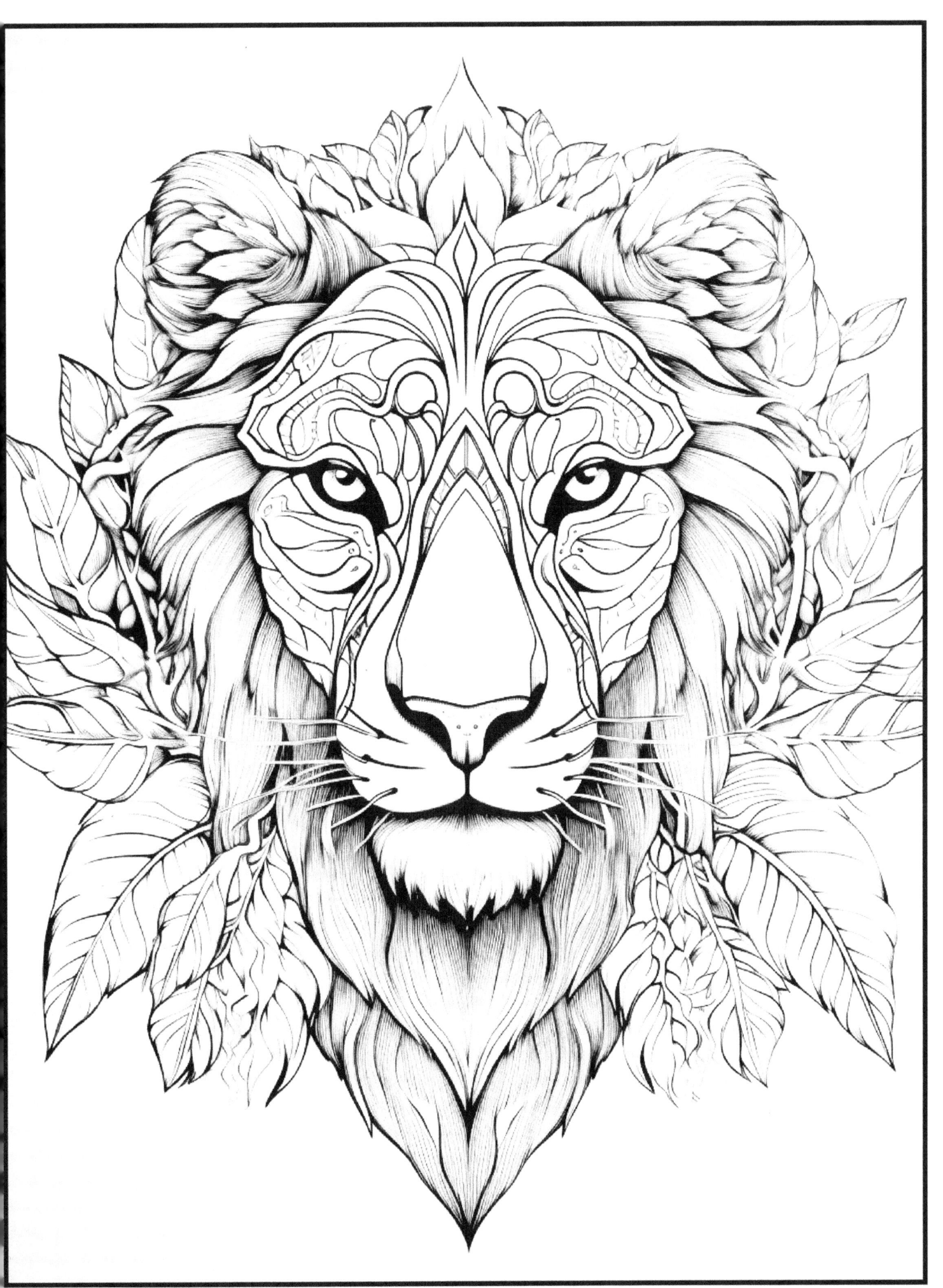

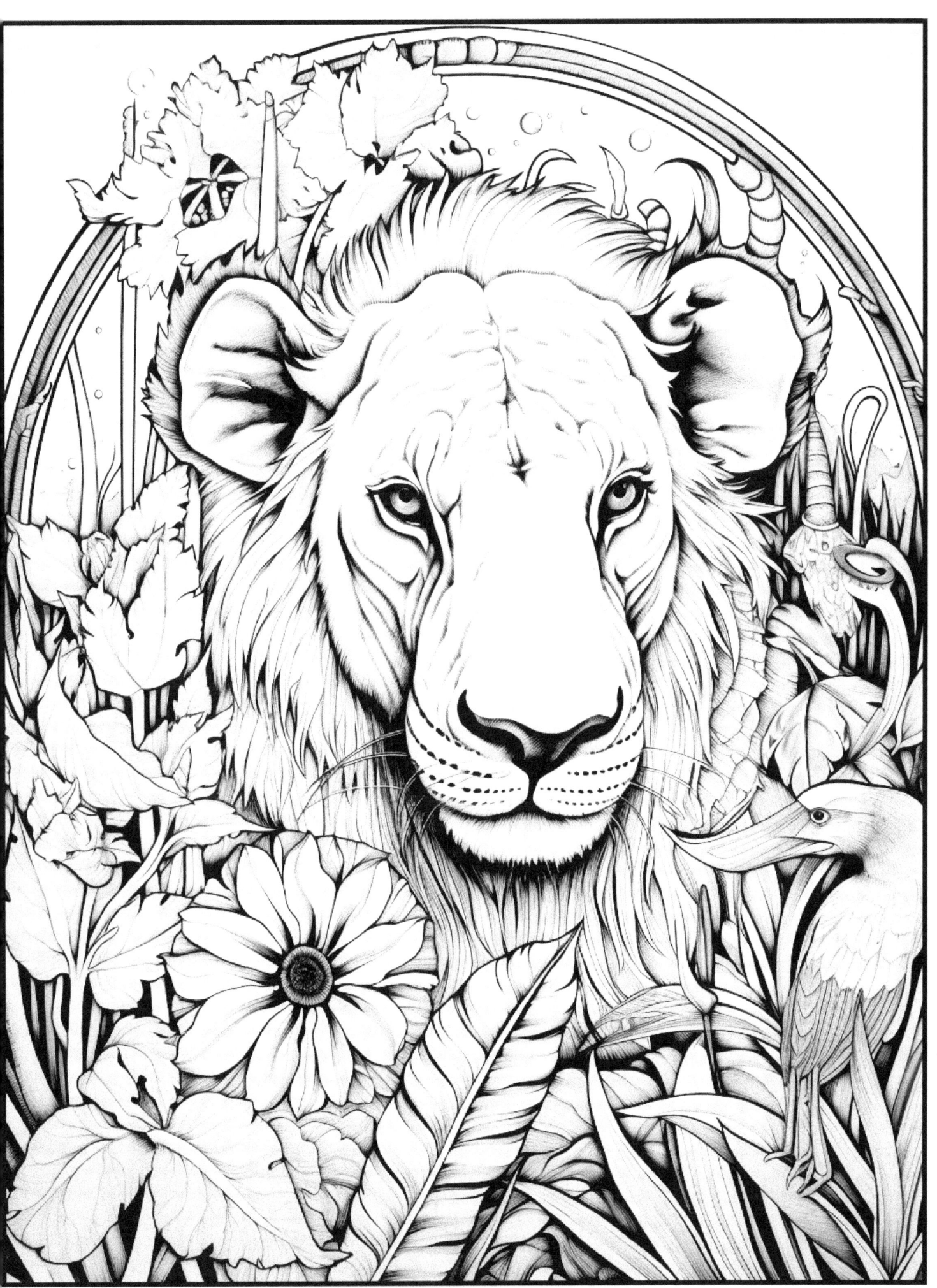

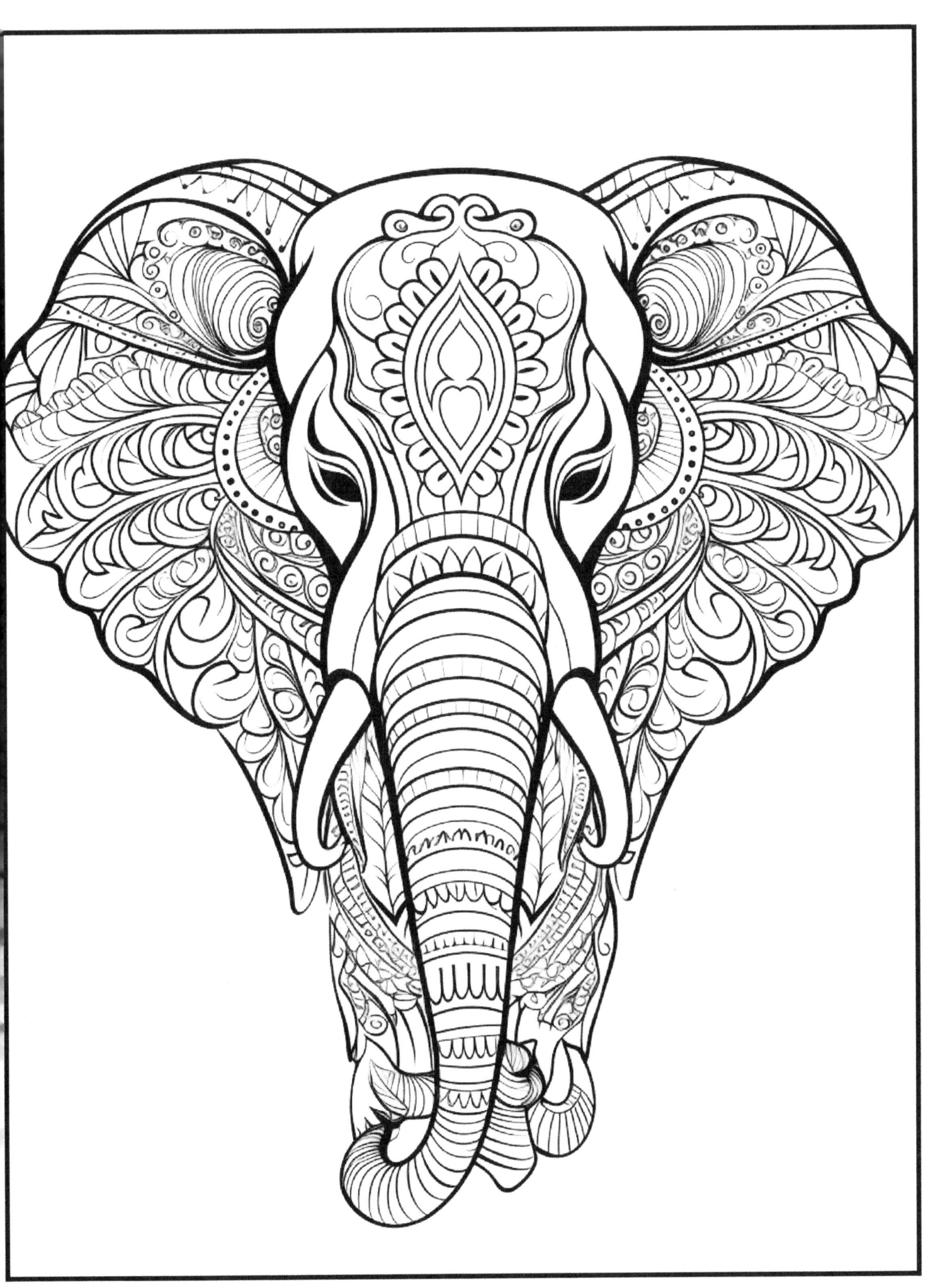

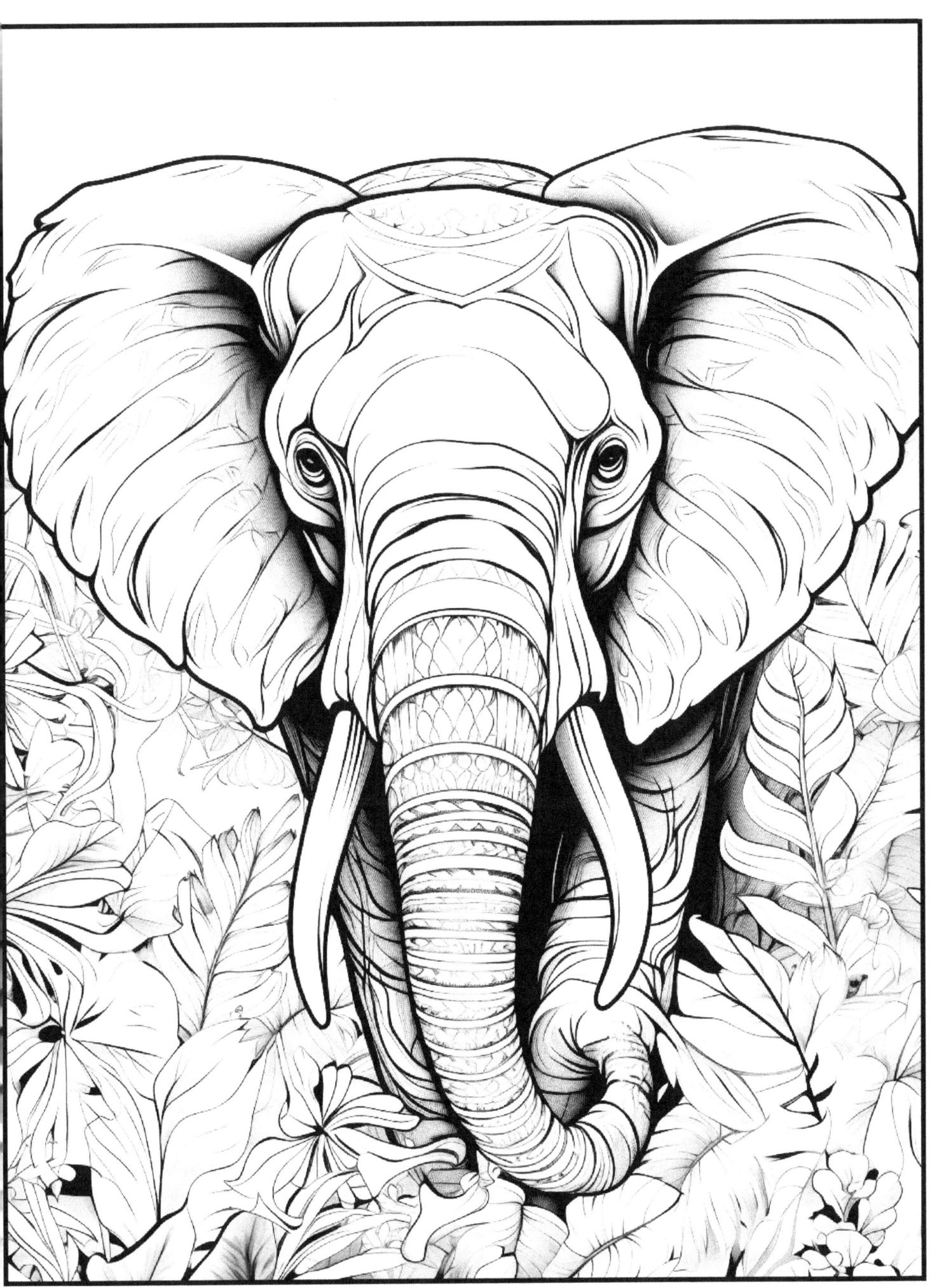

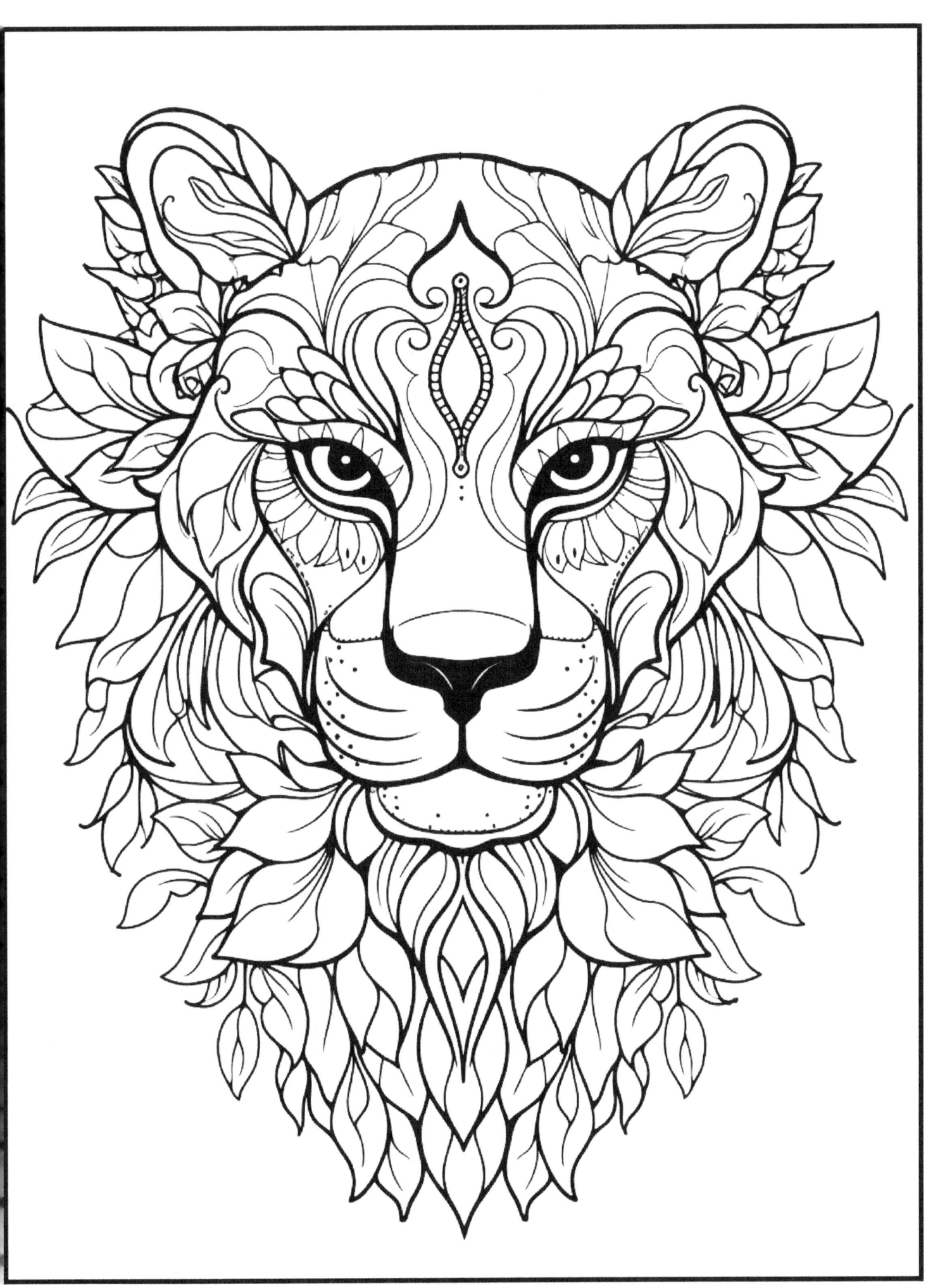

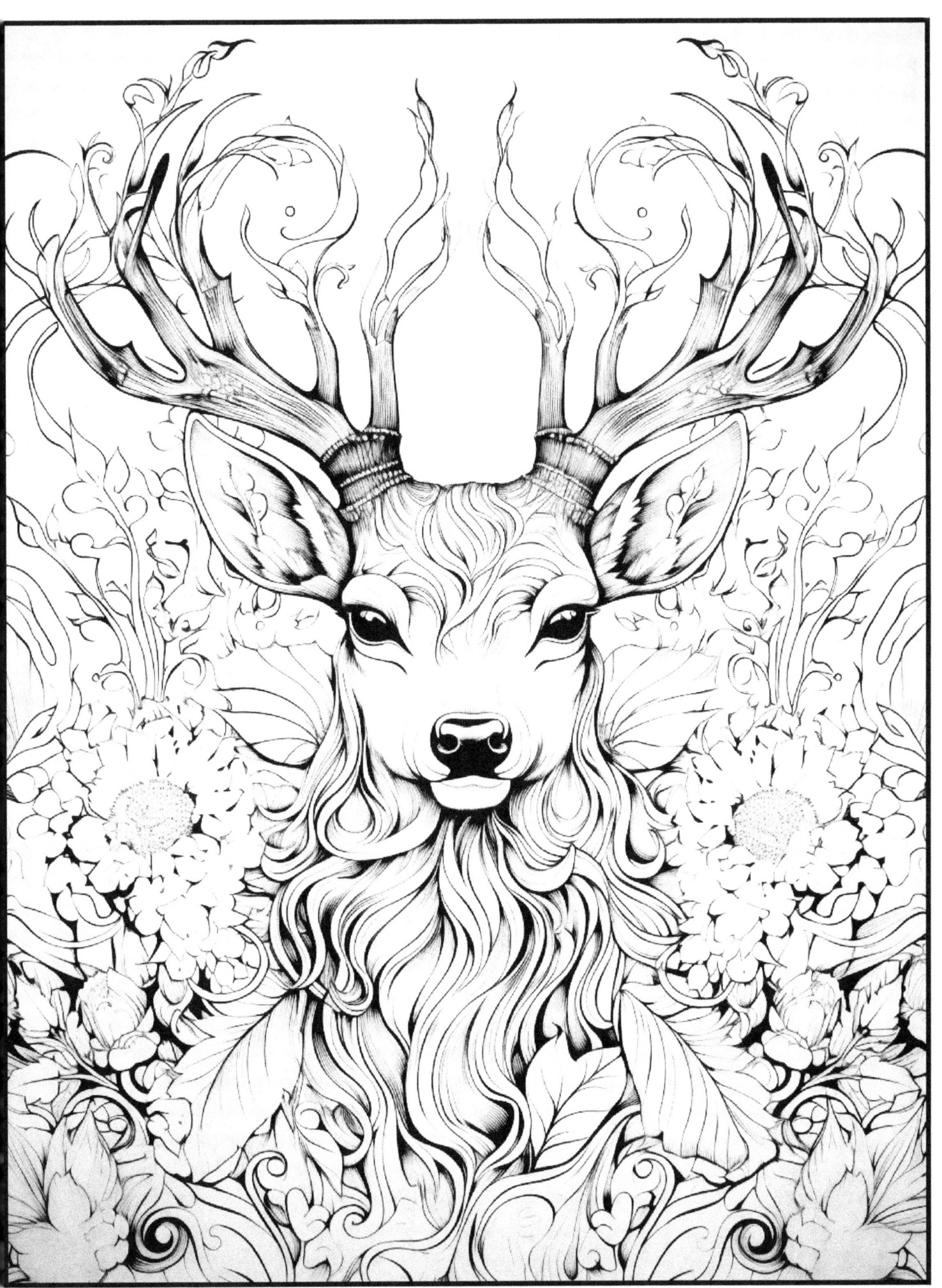

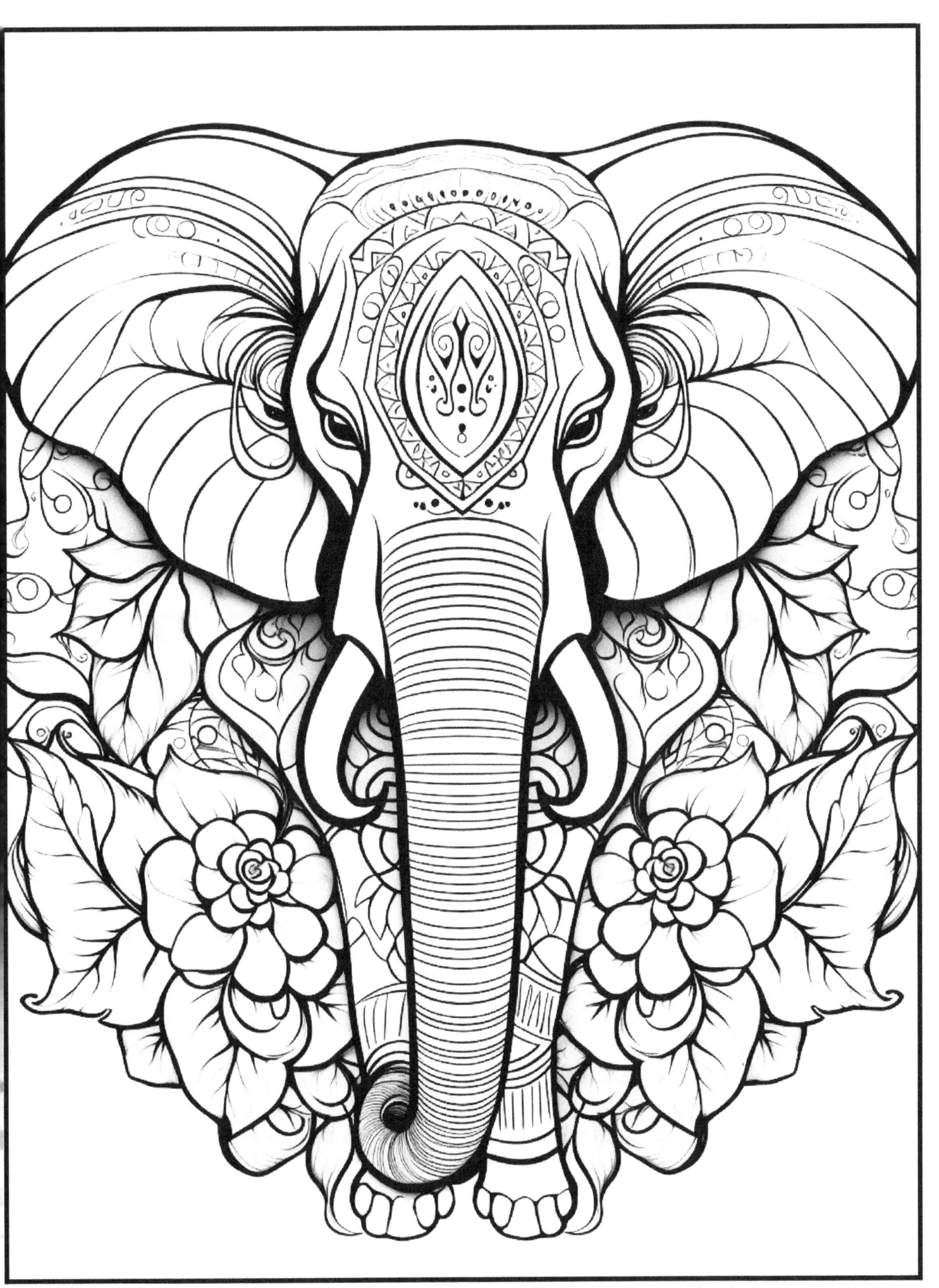

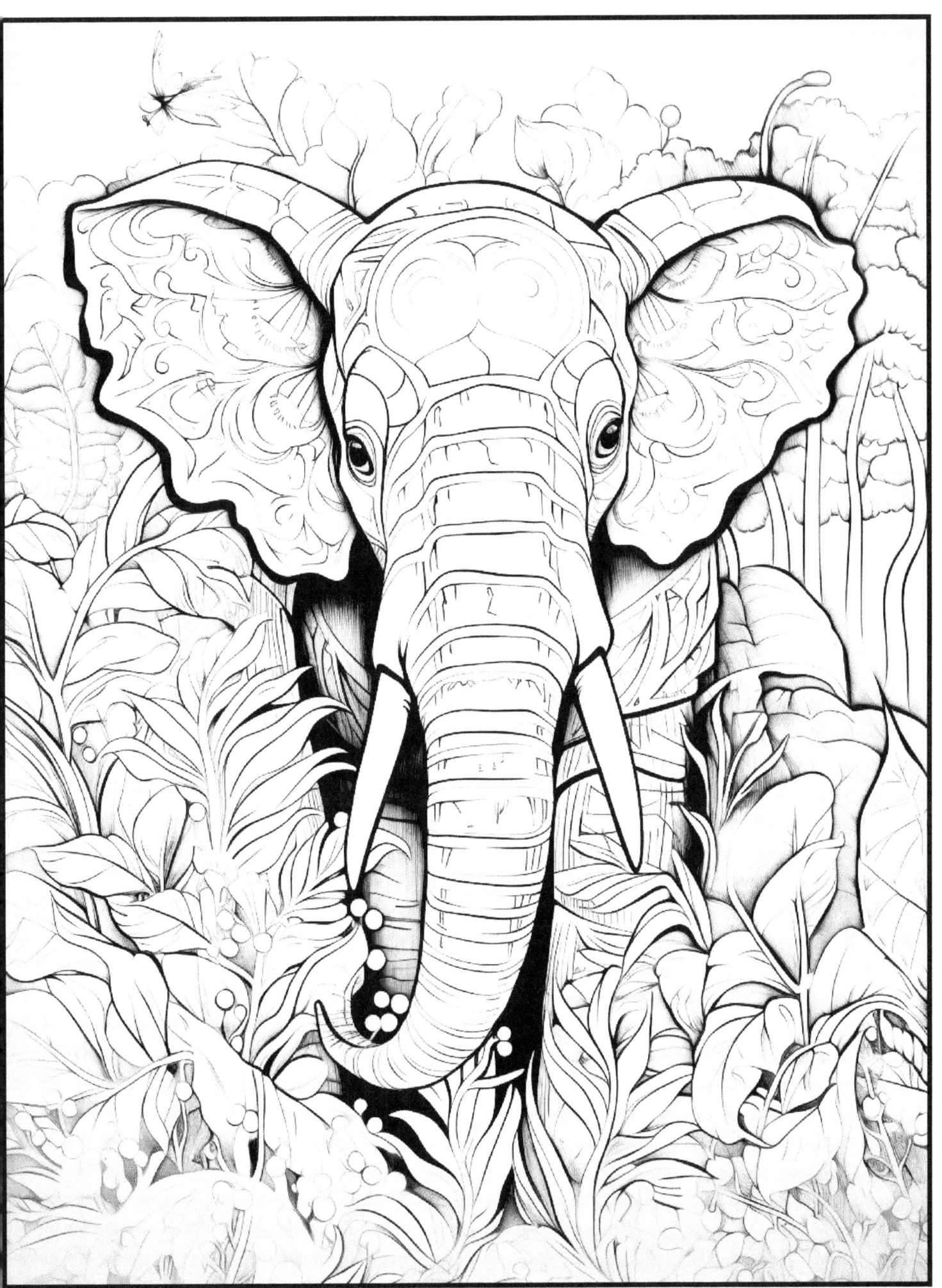

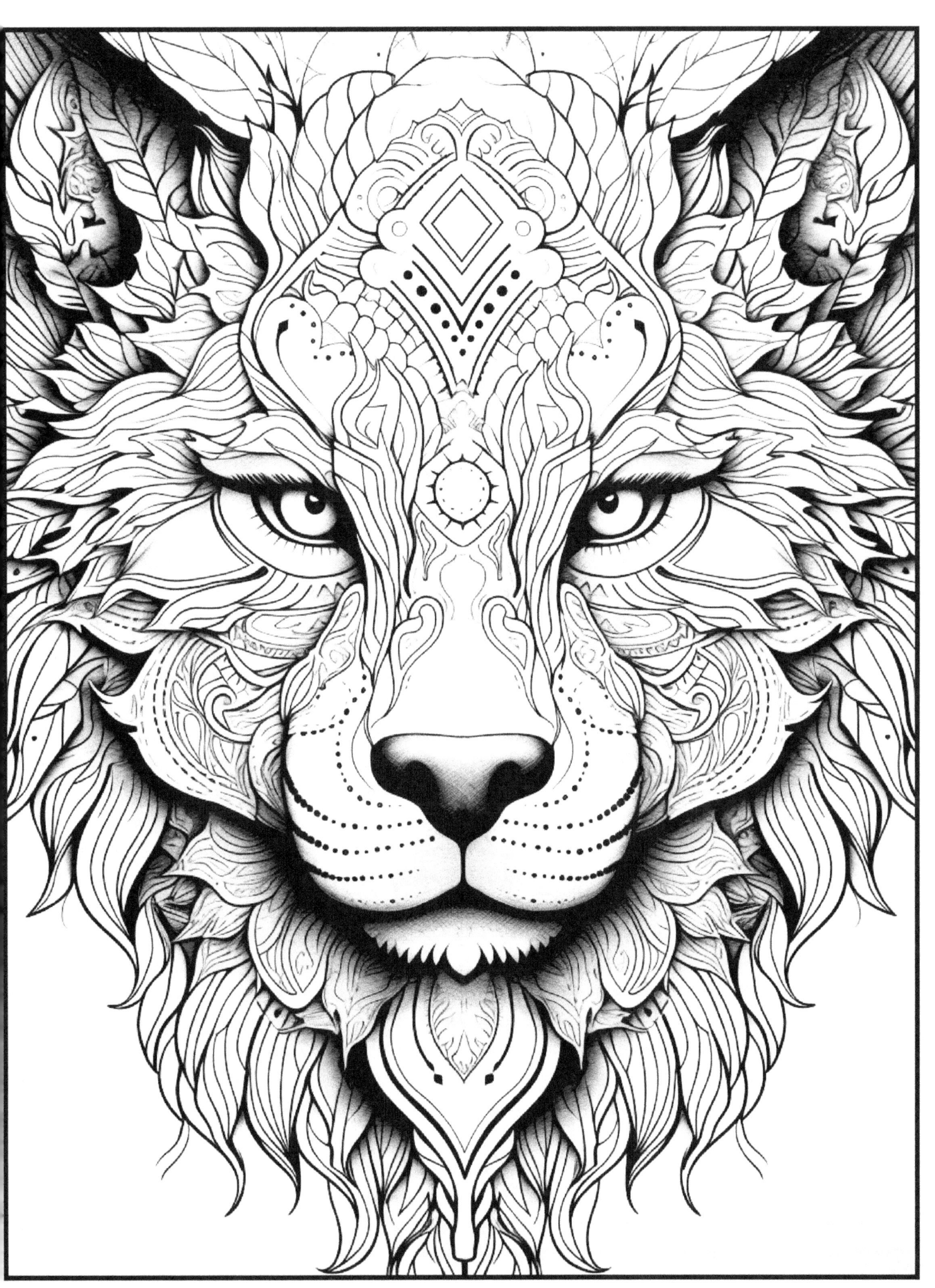

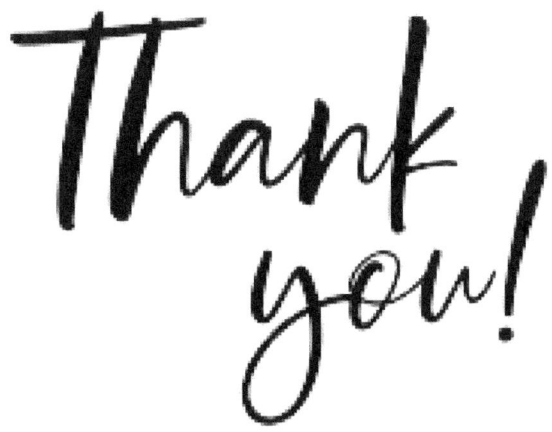

We thank you for your purchase. If you enjoyed this book, please consider writing us a review. A few seconds of your time makes a large impact to businesses like ours!

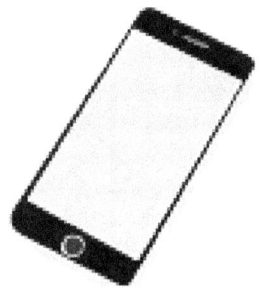

Electrifying Books

www.ingramcontent.com/pod-product-compliance
Lightning Source LLC
Chambersburg PA
CBHW062109220526
45471CB00010B/3663